The CORETTA SCOTT KING AWARDS BOOK

from Vision to Reality

Henrietta M. Smith, Editor

Coretta Scott King Task Force

Social Responsibilities Round Table

AMERICAN LIBRARY ASSOCIATION
CHICAGO AND LONDON, 1994

Acquisition Editor: Bonnie J. Smothers

Cover designed by Richmond A. Jones

Text designed by Dianne M. Rooney

Composition and film by Clarinda Company in 10/12 and
11/14 Stempel Garamond on XYVision system

Four-color 16-page insert printed on 70-pound Sterling Litho
Gloss

Text printed on 50-pound Halopaque, a pH-neutral stock, and
bound in 10-point C1S cover stock by Creative Printing
Service, Inc.

ISBN 0-8389-3441-2

*With gratitude, this volume is dedicated to
these visionary Founders*

Glyndon Flynt Greer
Mabel McKissick
John Carroll

CONTENTS

COLOR PLATES

FOREWORD

The year 1994 is the twenty-fifth anniversary of the Coretta Scott King Award. This is truly a historic occasion. While we celebrate the Coretta Scott King Award and what it means to libraries, books, and young people, we must not forget that the year 1994 also marks forty years since the passage of the historic *Brown vs. Board of Education* decision, which eradicated legally segregated schools in our country. It was this historic decision, coupled with Rosa Parks's bravery, that led African Americans, under the leadership of the Rev. Martin Luther King Jr., to declare war on segregation and discrimination by throwing off the shackles of bondage.

It was twenty-five years ago that Glyndon Flynt Greer, a school librarian with a vision, decided to bring to the attention of librarians, publishers, and educators the need to make the library world and the American public aware of books by and about African Americans. She and her colleagues, Mabel R. McKissick, John F. Carroll, Beatrice James, Roger McDonald, Ella Gaines Yates, and several others took steps toward giving public attention to the works of black authors and illustrators. The lack of promotion of books for young people with themes related to the black experience and the lack of recognition given to black authors and illustrators fostered the establishment of the Coretta Scott King Award Committee.

Over the years Mrs. Greer continued the leadership of the program, even though she had many frustrations and stumbling blocks put in her pathway. One such impediment was the scheduling of the Coretta Scott King Award breakfast, a key to the program. The American Library Association wanted to decide the time of the breakfast, desiring to change it from the "prime time" of Tuesday mornings, allowing more flexibility for scheduling ALA sponsored programs. And, too, it was the feeling of some in this early history that there were those who opposed the establishment of a minority award. Mrs. Greer telephoned me and asked, "E. J., what shall we do?" Having been one of the founding members of the Social Responsibilities Round Table (SRRT), I said to her, "Let us make the Coretta Scott King program a task force of the Social Responsibilities Round Table." Mrs. Greer agreed. I telephoned the SRRT coordinator, who welcomed the idea, and the rest of the story is history.

As I have said on many occasions, twenty-five years ago the Newbery and Caldecott Committees had not yet begun to honor the quality work of black authors and illustrators with their coveted awards. The Interracial Council for Children's Books was the only organization that fostered a program for bringing quality books about and by blacks to the attention of American libraries. In 1979, the Coretta Scott King Award became an official award of SRRT. When Mrs. Greer passed in 1980, she was able to rest in peace because SRRT had made the Coretta Scott King Award and the program a task force and it was to be continued under the aegis of this ALA unit. In 1982, the award became an official American Library Association award, one designed from its beginnings to honor Mrs. Coretta Scott King for her courage and determination to continue the work for peace and world brotherhood of a great American leader.

E. J. Josey, Past President
American Library Association

PREFACE

The genesis of the Coretta Scott King Award is truly an "In the beginning" story. Thanks to school librarian and founder Mabel McKissick of New London, Connecticut, aspects of the early history can now be made a matter of record. During the 1969 American Library Association Conference in Atlantic City, there was a chance meeting between Mabel McKissick and Glyndon Greer, a school librarian from Englewood, New Jersey, formerly from the New York public library system. The two were vying for a poster of the late Dr. Martin Luther King Jr., which was on display at the booth of publisher John M. Carroll. During the course of conversation both librarians discussed the fact that in the years since the Newbery and Caldecott Medals were in existence, neither of these awards had been presented to a minority author or illustrator. It is reported that Carroll then remarked, "Why don't you ladies start an award to do just that?" The idea was taken seriously!

As the idea evolved the three founders, Mabel McKissick, Glyndon Greer, and John Carroll, sought the aid and support of other librarians in the New Jersey area. Those active in this initial organizational move included Harriet Brown, New York City Board of Education; Beatrice James, president of the New Jersey Library Association; Roger McDonough, New Jersey State Librarian; and Ella Yates, assistant director of the Montclair, New Jersey, public library. The early decisions this group would have to make included a name for the award, an award winner, and a time and place for a presentation. Glyndon Greer suggested that the award be named for her friend Coretta Scott King, wife of the slain civil rights leader, Martin Luther King Jr. The purpose was "to commemorate the life and work of Martin Luther King Jr." and to honor his wife for her "courage and determination in continuing the work for peace and brotherhood."

The inaugural presentation was made during the May 1970 meeting of the New Jersey Library Association. At a gala dinner affair, Erma Burrell presented a plaque to the winning author, Lillie Patterson. Patterson was selected for having written her timely biography, *Martin Luther King, Jr., Man of Peace.* The cost of the plaque was underwritten by publisher John Carroll. The speaker for the occasion was Sylvia

Drew, daughter of the late Dr. Charles Drew, the physician and scientist whose pioneer research in the preservation of blood for later use in blood transfusions saved many lives during World War II.

The Garrard Publishing Company provided complimentary copies of the winning book for all who attended the program. The presentation was repeated at a small program held during the summer conference of the American Library Association, although at that time neither the award nor this pioneer band had received official recognition from ALA.

From this small beginning change was constant and progressive, and the founders worked to establish a more organized structure and to seek additional financial support to give the award more visibility. Visibility, it was felt, could also come if librarians from a wider geographical area were actively involved in the program. Correspondence was sent to librarians known to the pioneer group; and to facilitate getting together, meetings were held during ALA conferences. Among the new voices that became a part of the group were Dr. Virginia Lacy Jones, director of the Atlanta University library school; Augusta Baker and Barbara Rollock, New York public library system; Effie Lee Morris, now in the California library system; Dr. E. J. Josey, then in New Jersey and now at the University of Pittsburgh; and Basil Phillips, managing editor with the Johnson Publishing Company, Chicago.

It was not until 1972 that the award breakfast was held at an official ALA site. The award at this time was still not recognized as a part of the ALA Awards. Of historical interest is that in 1974 this fledgling group extended its recognition to include an illustrator award. The first such award went to George Ford for his illustrations in Sharon Bell Mathis's biography *Ray Charles*.

Books selected as winner and honor books in 1974 were the first to receive the Coretta Scott King Award Seal. Internationally known artist Lev Mills created a seal designed to embody Martin Luther King Jr.'s philosophy of peace and universal brotherhood. This concept is represented by a dove of peace, the symbols of various spiritual beliefs, and a child reading a book—recognizing knowledge as the key to understanding. The seal for the winning book is produced in bronze representing the skin tones of Mother Africa. Honor books receive a silver seal. Artist Lev Mills, who donated his time and talent to this project, is chair of the art department at Atlanta University. Visitors to Atlanta may see his work on a large scale in a mural at the Martin Luther King Jr. station of the Atlanta Rapid Transit System.

In 1980 through the perseverance and persuasion of Dr. E. J. Josey, the Coretta Scott King Task Force became a unit under the Social Responsibilities Round Table (SRRT). Glyndon Greer was named the

first chair of this now-official ALA body. Prior to this time the founders and supporters met *during* ALA but were not listed as a part of the ALA activities. Glyndon Greer was named chair of the Task Force. Sadly this was a short-lived appointment for Greer who died in August of 1980. In 1982 the ALA Council by resolution declared the Coretta King Award an official ALA award!

Glyndon Greer was succeeded as chair by Harriet Brown. Other chairpersons have included Effie Lee Morris, San Francisco, California; David Searcy, Atlanta, Georgia; Henrietta M. Smith, Delray Beach, Florida; and currently, Carolyn Garnes, Atlanta, Georgia.

Once firmly entrenched as a bona fide ALA award, the project underwent a series of significant changes. First, John Carroll suggested that SRRT take responsibility for the plaque that the winners received. Although his interest in the award never flagged, he felt that as a small publisher he could not afford to continue the contribution. And perhaps too, he felt that the award would take on a greater aura of prestige if sponsored by a large parent organization such as ALA rather than a small local donor. From the very beginning, the Johnson Publishing Company presented an honorarium to the winning author. Over time several companies or individuals donated the honorarium for the winning illustrator, including Coca-Cola Bottling Company, Walter Amos of Famous Amos Chocolate Chip Cookie Corporation, and entrepreneur M. E. Dare of Brooklyn, New York. Since 1980, Encyclopaedia Britannica has donated a set of encyclopedias to the winning author, and World Book has done the same for the winning illustrator.

Second, the group developed a clearly defined process for the selection of the Task Force chairperson. Bylaws were adopted that clearly delineated the responsibilities and eligibility for holding office both as the Task Force chair and for membership on the award-selection jury. Those serving in either of these categories must be members of the Social Responsibilities Round Table. Those interested in serving on the selection jury would need to be present at Task Force meetings before being eligible to be either nominated or appointed to the selection jury.

Third, a written criteria for selection has evolved over the years. As interest in the award has grown and more titles by African American authors and illustrators have been published, so has the jury continued to review and strengthen the criteria by which winning books are chosen. In the early days choices were decidedly limited, so one might note that a chosen book, although not written by an ethnic minority author, still represented the concepts of brotherhood and/or spoke to some aspect of the black experience. With the passage of time and with patience, professionally critical selectivity, and constant communication with publishers, a wide range of quality titles by African American authors and illustrators has resulted. It is from this group of books that the racially mixed jury makes its decisions. The present criteria state in part:

> Recipients are African American authors and illustrators whose distinguished books promote an understanding and appreciation of the culture and contribution of all people to the realization of the "American dream."

At the June 1993 ALA conference the ALA Award Committee accepted the Coretta Scott King Task Force's request to establish the Genesis Award. The award will be a certificate of recognition presented to an author or illustrator whose work shows significant promise. Criteria are modeled after the policies that govern the selection of the Coretta Scott King Award with the exception that the recipient may not have had more than three works published.

In 1989, to further publicize the Coretta Scott King Award, whose prestige was growing by leaps and bounds, the first full-color brochure was designed and produced by the ALA graphics department. The brochure displayed pictures of the covers of the current winning and honor books and included a cumulative list of titles from the award's inception. An updated brochure is available through ALA after each midwinter conference when winners and honor books are chosen.

Although the usual format of the award breakfast is a simple program, with acceptance speeches from the winning and honor authors and illustrators, there have been some special highlights. When it seemed appropriate, recognition plaques were given to those who were deemed to have rendered service above and beyond what anyone would ask. Over the years the recipients have been Frankcina Glass, author; Jean Coleman, SRRT coordinator when the Task Force became a unit; John Johnson, Johnson Publishing Company for years of financial support; Barbara Rollock, supervisor of children's services, New York Public Library; Coretta Scott King; Basil Phillips and Marion Sloan for personal involvement in award presentations; and John Carroll, founder.

In 1990 a special gift initiated yet another Coretta Scott King breakfast tradition—the children's table. From that time, individuals, publishers, and business corporations would send a check for the price of one or more tickets to the SRRT office. The local arrangements chair would then orchestrate getting children from the geographical area of the ALA conference to attend the breakfast. The number in attendance has ranged from twenty to fifty! Thanks to the generosity of the publishers of the winning and honor books, each child receives one or more books to take home as mementos of this special day.

Other intermittent memorable highlights of the award breakfasts include a commemorative slide presentation for the twentieth anniversary, produced by Carolyn Garnes of Atlanta, Georgia. Coretta Scott King attended the breakfast in 1984 and 1993, and daughter Yolanda King brought a stirring message in 1989. Rosa Parks gave warm greetings in 1991. Mabel McKissick memorialized John Carroll at the 1986 breakfast. On a lighter note, at an unforgettable 1986 breakfast held in a newly constructed hotel in New York, the lights went out during Virginia Hamilton's acceptance speech right at the part when she spoke of "slaves sneaking away in the darkness." And a few moments later, a part of the ceiling fell! Luckily no one was hurt, and this incident became a topic of conversation throughout the conference.

At these annual breakfasts, the Coretta Scott King Task Force plays host to 500 to 800 people—quite a jump from the fifty who attended the very first presentation in 1970.

As the Coretta Scott King Task Force looks toward the future, a major goal is to establish a permanent location for all the books that have received the prestigious Coretta Scott King Award. The selected location will make the books accessible for research and house them as a part of the cultural history of African Americans. Presently titles are housed in various sites in Atlanta, Georgia, at Alabama A & M University, and at the ALA offices.

Reflecting on the first twenty-five years, all who have been involved with the Coretta Scott King Award can look with pride on what has been accomplished. After a few moments of basking in justifiable pride, they must move on, remembering the past but knowing too that without steady work there is no future.

There are many people to whom thanks must go for assistance in the compilation of this retrospective bibliography: the authors; the illustrators, all of whom *contributed* their artwork; those who sent photographs and biographical information; and the publishers who expedited clearing all copyright concerns and helped in many other ways.

Acknowledgment and special appreciation go to the writing team responsible for the annotations and biographical sketches that are the body of this work: Rita Auerbach, Carol Edwards, Kathleen Horning, Ann Miller.

Special thanks to Bonnie Smothers for her editorial advice, design leadership, creative production ideas, and gently firm way of helping us make an almost perfect product. And finally, thanks to Mattye Nelson, director of the Social Responsibilities Office, who continuously and cheerfully assured all of us that this project would come to *handsome* fruition.

Henrietta M. Smith

ACKNOWLEDGMENTS

Cover

Art by Jacob Lawrence

"In the North the Negro had better educational facilities." From the series The
    Migration of the Negro (1940–41).
Tempera on gesso on composition board, 12″ × 18″.
The Museum of Modern Art, New York. Gift of Mrs. David M. Levy.
Photograph © 1994 The Museum of Modern Art, New York.
(Reproduced in the children's book, *The Great Migration: An American Story*,
    by Jacob Lawrence, published by The Museum of Modern Art, New
    York, the Phillips Collection, and HarperCollins Publishers, 1993.)

Art from Award Winning Illustrations

Aïda. Courtesy of Leo and Diane Dillon and Harcourt Brace, Jovanovich,
    1990.

Beat the Story Drum, Pum-Pum. Courtesy of Ashley Bryan and Atheneum
    Books for Children, 1980.

Black Child. Courtesy of Peter Magubane, photographer, and Alfred A.
    Knopf, Publishers, 1982.

Brown Honey in Broomwheat Tea. Courtesy of Floyd Cooper and Harper-
    Collins, Publishers, 1993.

C.L.O.U.D.S. Courtesy of Pat Cummings and Lothrop, Lee and Shepard
    Books, 1986.

The Invisible Hunter: A Legend from the Miskito Indians of Nicaragua. Cour-
    tesy of JoeSam. and Children's Book Press, 1987.

Little Eight John. Courtesy of Wil Clay and Lodestar Books, 1992.

Mufaro's Beautiful Daughters. With the approval of the estate of John Steptoe.
    Courtesy of Lothrop, Lee and Shepard Books, 1987.

Nathaniel Talking. Courtesy of Jan Spivey Gilchrist and Black Butterfly Press,
    1989.

The Origin of Life on Earth: An African Creation Myth. Courtesy of Kathleen
    A. Wilson and Sight Productions, 1992.

Ray Charles. Courtesy of George Ford and Crowell Publishers, 1973.

Soul Looks Back in Wonder. Courtesy of Tom Feelings and Dial Books for Young Readers, 1993.

Sukey and the Mermaid. Courtesy of Brian Pinkney and Four Winds Press, 1992.

The Talking Eggs. Courtesy of Jerry Pinkney and Dial Books for Young Readers, 1989.

Tar Beach. Courtesy of Faith Ringgold and Crown Publishers, 1991.

Uncle Jed's Barbershop. Courtesy of James Ransome and Simon & Schuster Publishers, 1993.

Under the Sunday Tree. Courtesy of Mr. Amos Ferguson and Harper & Row Publishers, 1988.

Working Cotton. Courtesy of Carole Byard and Harcourt Brace Jovanovich, Publishers, 1992.

Photographs used with biographical sketches courtesy of the publishers or by special photographers as noted.

Literary Permissions

Excerpts from "A Conversation with Patricia McKissack" by Rudine Sims Bishop in *Language Arts* 69, no. 1 (Jan. 1992): 70–74. Used by permission of NCTE and Patricia McKissack.

Poem by Langston Hughes, "Merry Go Round," copyright 1959 by Langston Hughes and renewed 1987 by George Houston Bass. Reprinted by permission of Alfred A. Knopf, Inc.

Excerpts from "Pat Cummings, Artist" by Rudine Sims Bishop in *Language Arts* 70 (Jan. 1993): 53–59. Used by permission of NCTE and Pat Cummings.

I'm shaking off the old skin and I'll leave it here in the hole. I'm coming out, no less invisible without it, but coming out nevertheless. . . .
Who knows but that, on the lower frequencies, I speak for you?

Ralph Ellison, Invisible Man

Writing is just a different name for conversation—

Laurence Sterne

Author Awards

Maya Angelou
Pearl Bailey
James Berry
Clarence N. Blake
Candy Dawson Boyd
Ashley Bryan
Terri Bush
Alice Childress
Shirley Chisholm
Lucille Clifton
Louise Crane
Ossie Davis
Alexis De Veaux
Alfred Duckett
Mari Evans
William J. Faulkner
Elton Fax
Carol Fenner
Frankcina Glass
Berry Gordy Sr.
Lorenz Graham
Shirley Graham
Eloise Greenfield
Barney Grossman
Virginia Hamilton
Joyce Hansen

James Haskins
Kristin Hunter
Angela Johnson
June Jordan
Julius Lester
Lessie Jones Little
Donald F. Martin
Sharon Bell Mathis
Fredrick McKissack
Patricia C. McKissack
Mary E. Mebane
Walter Dean Myers
John Nagenda
Lillie Patterson
Margaret Peters
Jeanne Whitehouse Peterson
Sidney Poitier
Dorothy Robinson
Charlemae Rollins
Ellease Southerland
Ruth Ann Stewart
Mildred D. Taylor
Joyce Carol Thomas
Janice May Udry
Mildred Pitts Walter

From *Toning the Sweep*

I left the desert and my mama when I was seventeen years old and angry. One morning I told Ola I was moving to San Francisco. She stared at me for a few seconds before she started packing me a bag of fruit for the trip.

She was as tired of fighting as I was when she put me on the Greyhound going north. When the bus took off, I pressed my face against the window and cried. Ola followed that bus for five miles down the dusty desert road. She gave me every chance to change my mind and stop the bus, but I didn't.

—Angela Johnson

1994 WINNER

Johnson, Angela. *Toning the Sweep.* Orchard, 1993. 103 p.

Toning the Sweep, a cross-generational story, gloriously celebrates Grandma Ola's life even as that life, ravaged by cancer, is quietly slipping away. Fourteen-year-old Emily and her mother, Diane, have come to the desert to help Ola pack, bid farewell to her beloved desert, and move to spend the rest of her life with family in Cleveland. The sunshine yellow of Ola's house seems symbolic of the joy and warmth that overshadows the impending sense of loss.

Using a camcorder, Emily videotapes Ola with each of her friends. She records their laughter and the repetition of oft-told stories of people long gone. She makes a memory of their tragedies, dreams, and hopes so many times gone unfulfilled. The camera records the reason for her mother's quiet anger against the Ola that Emily loves and brings a stronger understanding to their mother-daughter relationship. As Emily listens to Ruth and David and to Aunt Martha and all the other "aunts," she becomes aware of their philosophical approach to life that makes them as relentlessly enduring as the Arizona desert they call home. And the lives are not recorded in isolation. Emily photographs the lizards, the plants, and the trees that are the natural background of this arid place.

Readers will be intrigued to learn the poignant meaning of toning the sweep and its significance in the life of Emily and her mother. Written in poetic prose and touched lightly with humor, this is an unforgettable story steeped with emotions that will linger with the reader long beyond the final page.

HONOR

Myers, Walter Dean. *Malcolm X: By Any Means Necessary.* Il. with black-and-white photographs. Scholastic, 1993. 210 p.

The dramatic opening chapter tells of Malcolm X's deceptively quiet confrontation with the police in Harlem and introduces readers to the multifaceted

From *Malcolm X*

Malcolm spoke for the voiceless, for the people from whom not even some black leaders wanted to hear. He spoke for the jobless, and for the homeless. He spoke for the young men whose hard bodies, bodies that could perform miracles on inner-city basketball courts, were not wanted in America's offices. He spoke for the millions of black Americans who saw themselves as a minority in a world in which most of the inhabitants were people of color like themselves. He spoke for the men and women who had to turn too many other cheeks, had to fight off too many insults with nothing but smiles.

—Walter Dean Myers

life of a man who left an indelible mark on contemporary American history. Myers provides an in-depth picture of the early years of Malcolm X, born Malcolm Little. He introduces Malcolm's father, an outspoken minister and civil rights leader in the depression era. The author presents vivid pictures of Malcolm's poverty-stricken childhood after the death of his beloved father and of his mother's slow and tragic mental breakdown that resulted in the disintegration of the Little family. Myers does not gloss over Malcolm Little's academic prowess and brilliant mind, which in his youth was often used to make a flashy but less than savory living. The author describes Malcolm Little's six years of imprisonment during which he was introduced to the principles and philosophy of Islam, a factor that was a turning point in the life of the man who became Malcolm X. And this astute author does not fail to explain to young readers the meaning of "X" as explained by Malcolm X's mentor, Muslim leader Elijah Muhammad. "X" we learn signifies the eradication of the surname that slaves were given based on their master's name. It was symbolic of the irrevocable loss of the name given in Mother Africa.

The book includes sidelights of African American history relevant to the development of Malcolm X's personality, including the Marcus Garvey movement, the heroic work of the 54th Massachusetts Regiment of Civil War fame, the Anthony Burns slave case, and Malcolm X's interaction with Fidel Castro, among others.

With quiet compassion Myers discusses Malcolm X's gradual change from total hatred of the white man—and disparaging view of Martin Luther King Jr.'s nonviolent approach to racial equality—to a man who realized that there was wisdom in being willing to accept people as individuals. This awakening came after his 1964 pilgrimage to Mecca. It marked the beginning of a negative change in the relationship between Malcolm X and Elijah Muhammad, one that many feel may have led to this outspoken leader's assassination in 1965.

With consummate skill, Myers has written the story of a complex personality in tones that make this important life accessible to young adult readers. The book is further enriched with a bibliography that includes books and periodicals covering the early 1930s to the present.

Thomas, Joyce Carol. *Brown Honey in Broomwheat Tea.* Il. Floyd Cooper. HarperCollins, 1993. unp.

The poems in this outstanding collection speak in many voices: a plea for acceptance in "Cherish Me"; cautionary wariness in the title piece, "Brown Honey in Broomwheat Tea"; and the strength that is an integral part of African American heritage in "Becoming the Tea."

> But like the steeping brew
> The longer I stand
> The stronger I stay.

Thomas's rhythmic patterns, image-filled language, and provocative themes evoke a wide range of emotions. Although perhaps particularly attuned to the African American heritage, the ideas are worthy of contemplation and reflection by readers regardless of their ethnic heritage.

1993 WINNER

McKissack, Patricia C. *The Dark-Thirty: Southern Tales of the Supernatural.* Il. Brian Pinkney. Knopf, 1992. 122 p.

Patricia McKissack has written a collection of stories made for reading aloud or for telling "at that special time when it is neither day nor night and when shapes and shadows play tricks on the mind." There is a well-balanced mix of the humorous, the ghostly, and the supernatural among the ten entries. Readers will probably make individual choices among topics such as the story of the Pullman porter who tried to avoid the 11:59, known as the death train, but answered its call on a gloomy night; the story of the slave who took a lesson from the wasps in making a wise decision to disobey his master; or perhaps join in the fun of mastering the monster in the tale of the chicken coop. Each story is introduced with a historical note giving its foundation or origin. Brian Pinkney's scratch-board illustrations are a fitting complement to the mood of the stories.

From *The Dark-Thirty*

The Dark-Thirty: Southern Tales of the Supernatural is a collection of original stories rooted in African American history and the oral storytelling tradition. They should be shared at that special time when it is neither day nor night and when shapes and shadows play tricks on the mind. When you feel fear tingling in your toes and zinging up your spine like a closing zipper, you have experienced the delicious horror of a tale of the dark-thirty.

—Patricia C. McKissack

HONOR

Walter, Mildred Pitts. *Mississippi Challenge.* Bradbury, 1992. 205 p.

Mississippi Challenge is a documented study of a state whose historical treatment of African Americans is memorable for its cruelty and inhumanity. With candor, Walter traces freedom movements past and present and details the triumphs and failures of citizens who fought and died for justice: the sit-ins of the sixties, the often fatal attempts at voter registration, and the inequalities in educational expenditures, which fostered the establishment of the freedom schools.

Blended into the text on contemporary affairs is a careful study of the early history of the state, the lives of some of the leaders, and little-known facts about nineteenth-century African American political leaders. This material helps youthful readers to link the past with the present.

Black-and-white photographs and personal interviews extend the information in this historically based reference. A scholarly bibliography provides reference sources for further research.

McKissack, Patricia C., and Fredrick McKissack. *Sojourner Truth: Ain't I a Woman.* Scholastic, 1992. 186 p.

The McKissacks' stirring biography has captured the strength, the steadfastness, and the perseverance of a powerful woman determined to be free. There are engrossing details of Sojourner Truth's efforts to keep her family together, to save the life of her wayward son, Peter, and to escape from the deceit of two "religious" charlatans. Meticulous research documents events in Sojourner Truth's life as she traveled in places where others dared not go, speaking out against slavery and fighting for *all* women's rights at a time when this was the calling of only a select few—and these mainly men. In a slavery dispute, for example, Sojourner Truth is recorded to be the first black woman to defeat a white man in a court of law. There was rapt attention when this imposing figure, over six feet tall, spoke with moving dignity. In answer to a minister's charge about her womanhood Truth responded:

> I have ploughed and I have planted. And I have gathered into barns, and no man could head me . . . I have borne children and seen them sold into slavery when I cried out in a mother's grief none heard me but Jesus—and ain't I a woman.

This moving biography is enriched with interesting photographs and a very special section of brief biographical sketches of personalities, white and black, who were a part of Sojourner Truth's memorable life.

Myers, Walter Dean. *Somewhere in the Darkness.* Scholastic, 1992. 168 p.

With a strikingly significant title, Myers sets the focus of this dramatic story. Somewhere in the darkness a father is trying to establish a relationship between himself and the son he abandoned at an early age. On a dark night Crab, just escaped from prison, shows up at his teenaged son's home. He abruptly tells guardian Mama Jean that he has come to claim his son. With this, Crab and Jimmy begin a cross-country trek during which Jimmy learns *who* his father is—an escapee, a con man, a womanizer, but still a man who wants

From *Somewhere in the Darkness*

"How you doing!"

The voice startled Jimmy. He turned to see a tall,
thin man leaning against the wall.

"Doing okay," Jimmy said, trying to lower his voice
so he would seem older.

"Your name is Little, isn't it?" the man asked.

"Yeah," Jimmy said. "Who you?"

"I'm your father," the man replied.

—Walter Dean Myers

to be a father to his son. Just before Crab's death there is that moment of reconciliation and the poignancy of that moment in which Jimmy realizes he has learned from Crab the kind of father he himself wants to be.

Jimmy thought about his having a child. It seemed so far off, like something that could never happen, but somehow would. He thought about what he would do with the child if it were a boy. He wouldn't know much about getting money to buy food for him or what thing to tell him to do except to be good and not get into trouble. But he would tell him all the secrets he knew, looking right into his eyes and telling him nothing but the truth so that every time they were together they would know things about each other. That way there would be a connection . . . something that would be there even when they weren't together. He would know . . . where their souls touched and where they didn't.

Somewhere in the Darkness speaks to all who are parents and those who someday will be.

1992 **WINNER**

Myers, Walter Dean. *Now Is Your Time! The African American Struggle for Freedom.* HarperCollins, 1991. 292 p.

In his first nonfiction book, Walter Dean Myers brings to audiences of all ages a memorable history of African Americans that spans over four centuries. The opening chapters share with readers an aspect of African history often omitted in most history texts—the time of high culture, noble rulers, great centers of learning, and scholars such as Ibrahima, whose knowledge brought students from all directions to learn from him. Scholarly research, personal interviews with the descendants of those captured and brought in chains to this country, and carefully selected photographs from historical collections are the foundation of a book that eloquently tells the story of African Americans who achieved in spite of hardships. Myers's prose is moving and convincing; the interviews add a sense of the contemporary. There seems to be a challenge to young readers in the very choice of the title, *Now Is Your Time!* Like Myers, may those who share this masterpiece of American history move forward strengthened by the author's words of celebration:

> I claim the darkest moments of my people and celebrate their perseverance.
> I claim the joy and the light and the music and the genius and the muscle and the glory of these I write about . . . and of the legions who have passed this way without yet having their stories told.

HONOR

Greenfield, Eloise. *Night on Neighborhood Street.* Il. Jan Spivey Gilchrist. Dial, 1991. unp.

From dusk to deep into the night these seventeen poems celebrate life in the neighborhood at that special time when work is done. Sleepovers, crying babies, church meetings, and "Fambly Time," the child fearful of the dark, and kids playing on the street corner are all depicted. Gouache paintings highlighted with pastels accompany the poetry. Greenfield recognizes the many temptations toward wrong-doing that often accompany nighttime yet shows that the community can cope by uniting and offering "warmth and life" to undo the attractions of "The Seller" and others who want to harm its inhabitants. Powerful words offer comfort and solace to children with rhythms and images that soften the darkness's ability to frighten. Night becomes friend instead of nightmare.

1991 WINNER

Taylor, Mildred D. *The Road to Memphis.* Dial, 1990. 290 p.

Cassie Logan's personal courage serves her well during a dangerous trip she makes from Mississippi to Tennessee in 1941 with her brother Stacey and his friends in Stacey's new car. Out on the open highway, the four African American teenagers, far from the protection of their families and their community, face unknown hazards at every turn in the road. This gripping narrative re-creates the perilous tensions of that time and place, as Cassie crosses over an invisible boundary and suddenly finds herself traveling across the unfamiliar terrain of adulthood.

HONOR

Haskins, James. *Black Dance in America: A History Through Its People.* Il. with photographs. HarperCollins, 1990. 232 p.

Brief biographical passages about individual African American dancers are chronologically arranged and connected by descriptions of the dances they invented or refined, providing an accessible overview of this distinctive art form. Haskins also provides a social and historical context by showing the ways black dance influenced and was influenced by dance in general.

Johnson, Angela. *When I Am Old with You.* Il. David Soman. Orchard, 1990. unp.

In this warm, cross-generational story, the reader meets a child and his grandfather sharing hours of comfortable enjoyment. As they play cards, go fishing, enjoy a quiet picnic, or meet with friends at a lively party, the little boy muses that these are the things they will do together when *he* is as old as his grandfather. There is a moment of nostalgic sadness when the two are looking at the family album and each sheds tears for a different reason. One of the most endearing lines in the book is the one in which the little boy, totally unaware of age differences, reflects on the idea that when he is old *with* his grandfather, they will sit each in his own rocking chair and "just talk about things." In word and picture *When I Am Old with You* speaks with simple eloquence of the innocence of childhood.

1990 WINNER

McKissack, Patricia C., and Fredrick McKissack. *A Long Hard Journey: The Story of the Pullman Porter.* Il. with photographs. Walker, 1989. 144 p.

The authors combined in-depth research from primary and secondary sources to provide an uncompromising account of the history of African Americans who worked as porters aboard George Pullman's luxury sleeping cars. While the first generation of porters were newly freed from enslavement and grateful for work, poor working conditions and mistreatment at the hands of management led succeeding generations to unite under the leadership of A. Philip Randolph in a struggle for better pay and fair treatment. Songs, stories, first-person accounts, and numerous black-and-white photographs accompany the narrative, which is unique in content.

HONOR

Greenfield, Eloise. *Nathaniel Talking.* Il. Jan Spivey Gilchrist. Black Butterfly Children's Books, 1988. unp.

Nathaniel is nine years old and his voice is strong in this collection of eighteen poems accompanied by black-and-white illustrations. In the rhythms of blues and rap this young male voice comes through strong and buoyant. Emotions fill the corners of the poems as Nathaniel reflects and raps about his life. His pride and strength are grounded in his family and his troubles, which he faces with confidence. Nathaniel springs to life, a vibrant, funny, clear-sighted human being.

Hamilton, Virginia. *The Bells of Christmas.* Il. Lambert Davis. Harcourt, 1989. 59 p.

An elegant tribute to the childlike anticipation of family Christmas observances takes place in 1890 in the Bell family home located on the historic

---

From *Nathaniel Talking*

I see my future . . .
not all the things around me . . .
I just see me
my serious man face
thinking . . .
my big Nathaniel me
moving through the world
doing good and unusual
things

—Eloise Greenfield

National Road near Springfield, Ohio. Told from the point of view of twelve-year-old Jason Bell, the story offers multiple references to independence, to travel across time and space, and to the historical period. An invigorating sense of this loving African American family's continuity combines with a warm expression of noncommercialized holiday joy.

Patterson, Lillie. *Martin Luther King, Jr., and the Freedom Movement.* Il. with photographs. Facts On File, 1989. 178 p.

Expanding this famous African American's civil rights image to that of the human rights leader who won the 1964 Nobel Peace Prize, Patterson's biography offers a reliable transition between juvenile and adult book accounts of the twentieth-century freedom fighter. The biography is illustrated with black-and-white photographs, maps, and freedom songs and includes an excellent annotated listing of further reading and a brief chronology.

1 9 8 9   WINNER

Myers, Walter Dean. *Fallen Angels.* Scholastic, 1988. 309 p.

Using Vietnam for the setting and U.S. teenagers as most of the characters, this landmark novel offers a logical, easy-to-follow story about the illogic of war. Seventeen-year-old Richie Perry is the African American protagonist whose medical papers don't catch up with him before he's shipped overseas. The war at home is revealed in letters the soldiers receive from friends and family; however, almost all of the episodes occur in the jungle during tedious hours of waiting, which are occasionally interrupted by minutes of sheer terror and chaos. Although author Myers never moralizes, a highly moral core is evident throughout the mesmerizing novel. Along with Richie Perry's humanity and bravery, this morality will be remembered long after readers finish the book.

Lord, let us feel sorrow for ourselves and all the angel warriors that fall . . .

Fallen Angels
—Walter Dean Myers

HONOR

Berry, James. *A Thief in the Village and Other Stories.* Orchard, 1987. 148 p.

The short stories in *A Thief in the Village* give the reader a picturesque glimpse into the day-to-day life of the people in a Jamaican village. The vignettes, which cover a range of emotions from sad to philosophical to humorous, sing with Berry's poetic prose. Among the children that Berry is "celebrating," we meet Becky who wants a bike so that she can ride with the Wheels-and-Brake Boys. Mum says girls don't do that, but with an "all's well that ends well" finish, Becky gets a bike and her widowed Mum gets a "boyfriend." Then there is the pathos in the story of young Gustus who, during a raging hurricane, nearly loses his life trying to save the banana tree that was marked as his personal birthright—he had hoped to make money from the sale of the fruit to buy shoes. His father did not understand this concern until Gustus's near fatal accident as he returns to his storm-torn home and is felled by the tree. In the title story, a sister and brother, Nenna and Man-Man, set up an all-night vigil to catch the thief who has been stealing their coconuts. *A Thief in the Village* is a charming look at the people who live and work in a tropical village that is not always a paradise.

From *A Thief in the Village and Other Stories*

Boys and men sway in the warm sea, giving our animals a good Sunday scrub with bushy siroce vines. And we don't just scrub them. We get on their backs. We turn their heads to sea and give them a great swim out. Like ourselves, horses and mules love this. Like myself, they know this event means no work today. No work means it must be Sunday. And by this time even men and women who don't have work animals swarm down and make a big sea-bathing flock in the water. And the scene is Sunday wonderful! It's like a village baptism of people and animals. Not surprising, truly, we all come out of the sea feeling baptized, brighter, more cheerful, and more spirited.

—James Berry

Hamilton, Virginia. *Anthony Burns: The Defeat and Triumph of a Fugitive Slave.* Knopf, 1988. 193 p.

Biography and historical fiction are interwoven in a carefully written account of Anthony Burns's 1854 Boston trial based on the controversial federal Fugitive Slave Act. Documented from primary sources, the biographical portions concerning Burns's imprisonment and trial are interspersed with innovative fictional segments reconstructing his youth as an enslaved child in Virginia. Source notes, a list of persons in the book, excerpts from the Fugitive Slave Act, and the author's comments further increase the value of this unusual, illuminating book.

1988 WINNER

Taylor, Mildred D. *The Friendship.* Il. Max Ginsburg. Dial, 1987. 53 p.

In a powerful short story issued as a single volume, the four Logan children are witnesses to a frightening scene at the general store in Strawberry, Mississippi. When a respected elder in the African American community dares to call the white store owner by his first name, the elder is brutally attacked by a group of white men who are unaware of a decades-long friendship between the two. Mr. Tom Bee refuses to be cowed by the attack, however, and he continues to call out the name of the store owner even after he is lying on the ground, bleeding. Both literally and figuratively, this deeply moving story shows children a courageous model of active resistance to racism and oppression.

HONOR

De Veaux, Alexis. *An Enchanted Hair Tale.* Il. Cheryl Hanna. Harper, 1987. 40 p.

Sudan's wonderful hair—"a fan daggle of locks and lions and lagoons"—sets him apart from other kids in his neighborhood, who tease him because he is different. Upset by their cruelty, he storms away and, far from home, stumbles upon a whole family of folks with enchanted hair who help him celebrate his differences. De Veaux's rhythmic text is full of pleasing rhyme and alliteration. Her imagery brilliantly conveys the mystery and magic of Sudan's hair. The poem is enhanced and extended by Cheryl Hanna's captivating black-and-white pencil drawings.

Lester, Julius. *The Tales of Uncle Remus: The Adventures of Brer Rabbit.* Introd. by Augusta Baker. Il. Jerry Pinkney. Dial, 1987. 151 p.

A new Uncle Remus emerges from Lester's creative reshaping of forty-eight Brer Rabbit stories from African American traditions into modified, contemporary Southern-black English. Storytelling specialist Augusta Baker's introduction speaks of the importance for contemporary children to hear these tales; Lester's foreword advises telling or reading the tales in one's own language. Occasional black-and-white drawings complement the high-spirited tales, and four watercolors are reproduced in full color on double-page spreads.

1 9 8 7 **WINNER**

Walter, Mildred Pitts. *Justin and the Best Biscuits in the World.* Lothrop, 1986. 122 p.

After the death of his father, ten-year-old Justin finds himself living in a home "surrounded" by women—his mother and his two sisters. There is constant conflict because Justin has very set ideas about what is or is not man's work. His room is always a mess, washing dishes is not on his list of masculine chores, and if he ever tries to cook anything the kitchen becomes a disaster. But Grandfather Ward comes to the rescue when he takes Justin to his home, a prosperous ranch in Missouri, where Justin learns several lessons about what it takes to be a man. These lessons include learning how to make a bed, clean the kitchen, and make prize-winning biscuits. But for Justin and all the readers there is another reward: Walter shares a history of the contributions of black cowboys and through the grandfather's narration of his family history, a lesson in the importance of knowing who you are and where you come from. A moving moment is one in which Justin learns that it is even all right for a man to cry. Grandfather explains his tears and shares this proverb:

> The brave hide their fears but share their tears. Tears bathe the soul.

Walter has written a well-paced story with several levels of historical and social information.

HONOR

Bryan, Ashley, *Lion and the Ostrich Chicks and Other African Folk Tales.* Atheneum, 1986. 87 p.

See entry in 1987 honor books for illustration.

Hansen, Joyce. *Which Way Freedom?* Walker, 1986. 120 p.

> You born a man, not a slave—that the thing to remember. You got to learn which way freedom be. "It here first," he said, touching his own creased forehead, "in your mind."

Some 200,000 African Americans fought in the Civil War. The figure is real but too large to encompass all of their stories in a single story. By creating one fictional representative of the 200,000, Joyce Hansen brings this impersonal statistic to life.

We meet Obi as a nineteen- or twenty-year-old Union soldier, an escaped slave with a haunting memory of his mother's cries as years earlier he was torn from her arms and sold off to a different master. In a flashback, Obi relives the years he spent after this separation from his mother as one of three young slaves on a small South Carolina tobacco farm. He was sustained during his youth by a vague plan to find his mother again on one of the Sea Islands and escape with her to Mexico. As his memories of her become cloudy, he relies on the old freed slave, Buka, to help him recall her appearance and remember the bitter tears that fell on deaf ears.

With the start of the Civil War, the pressures to harvest the tobacco crop increase, and with this so do the beatings that Obi must endure. When Obi learns that the farm and its slaves are about to be sold, he enlists Buka's help to finally realize his dream of escape. On the plantation, Obi, Easter, and young Jason were always fast friends. Because of the danger they would face in the escape attempt, Obi and Easter are forced to leave young Jason behind as they follow Buka's plans for the "journey." Easter and Obi finally part, each seeking a separate way to freedom.

The reader follows Obi's tense flight until the moment that opened the book, when Obi joined the advancing Union army and was assigned to the Sixth U.S. Artillery of Colored Troops. For the first time he could call himself by the name *he* wanted, Obidiah Booker (*Obidiah* meaning "first born" and *Booker* for his faithful counselor and friend, Buka). Was this the way to freedom?

Profile: A Conversation with Patricia McKissack

RUDINE SIMS BISHOP

Patricia McKissack was the closing speaker at the Children's Literature Assembly workshop at the 1990 NCTE Annual Convention in Atlanta. We set aside part of the afternoon of November 19 for lunch and a long, relaxed, informal conversation. Excerpts follow.

Would you begin by talking about how you got started writing for children?

I actually got started in third grade. I wrote a poem, and the teacher put it on the bulletin board and said she liked it. It was thrilling to have other people read and respond to something I had written, and I don't think that feeling ever left me. I was forever scribbling ideas and thoughts. I kept a journal; I've always kept a diary.

When I became a teacher, I was bothered by the lack of materials for African American children. I taught eighth grade, that very important age group where they're looking for self, especially in books. I wanted to give my kids Paul Laurence Dunbar. He's an American standard. My mother had recited Dunbar for me, and I grew up jumping double dutch to "Jump back, honey, jump back!" But his work wasn't in our anthologies, where my kids could get it. So I said, "OK, I'll write it myself." So I did, and that was one of my first books (*Paul Laurence Dunbar: A Poet to Remember*, Childrens Press, 1984). It was the first time I had disciplined myself to write a whole manuscript—beginning, middle, and end—with purpose. Of course, it didn't get published for many years.

From teaching, I went into editing. I was the children's book editor for Concordia Publishing, a religious publishing house in St. Louis. I was with them for 6 years, so I learned the industry from the inside. Then I decided I wanted to write professionally, but it was difficult to do that and also work

---

Language Arts 69, No. 1 (Jan. 1992): 70–74.

fulltime as an editor, so I had to make a career choice. I couldn't just break away and start writing because it takes a while to get enough books in print to make a living. So I continued to teach, but at the college level. I taught freshman composition, and oddly enough, it was much like teaching eighth-grade English. It was from there that I moved into writing.

Did you want to be a writer when you were a child?

Yes, but I was told black people couldn't do that—"Girl, you better take something you can do. You'd better be a teacher." Even in college I was steered toward getting a teaching certificate "so you can have something to do when you graduate." I love the teaching profession. When people ask me what I do, I still say, "I write, and I teach." Teaching is very much a part of me; it was my stepping stone to writing, and it continues to be. But it's limiting to be told that's all you can do. Perhaps they were wise at the time, but today I would be appalled if a teacher told a child that he or she can't make a living as a writer, because you can. It's hard work, but you can make a living. And we need more black voices; we need different points of view. Six or seven black writers cannot represent all the attitudes, all the characters, all the ways in which characters interact with one another. When my books come under criticism, I say, "Now wait. I am just one voice in the wilderness. If you don't like my books, then read Virginia Hamilton or Eloise Greenfield or someone else who is doing something different. But don't expect me to speak for everyone."

Do you have some idea why there aren't more black writers?

It's tough to make a living as a writer, and it has taken a long time to finally get people to recognize that there is a need for good books written by good black authors. Now we've reached a point where we have good black writers. I consider myself a good writer. I'm a craftsman; I can write about any subject. I choose, however, to write about the African American experience. But I don't want to be limited to that, and I'd fight to the tooth if I thought I were.

Let's go back to those diaries and journals you kept as a child.

Our home burned in January, 1968, and I lost my yearbook, my marriage album, all of the *stuff*. I had boxes of memorabilia that I had collected through school, and I lost every bit of it. People ask me what I missed most after the fire. My first son's baby pictures. Things that can't be replaced. My childhood diaries. Like most little girls, I used to write my feelings. It was amazing how many times I fell in and out of love. I would scribble a poem now and then, and after a trip, I would describe it—all the smells and sounds and tastes. I did enjoy doing that. There's still a part of me that mourns that loss.

Tell me a little about your growing up.

My parents divorced when I was young, but they were together for 10 years, so I really got to enjoy my father. I was a daddy's girl, and in many ways I guess I still am. I was very close to my grandparents on both sides. My grandmothers were best friends; they knew each other before my parents knew each other. The two of them knew I was deeply hurt by the divorce and that I didn't understand any of it, so they surrounded me with love. My mother moved from Kirkwood, a small town near St. Louis, to Nashville, and I grew up there in the projects in the bosom of this loving family. They just spoiled me rotten, especially my maternal grandfather, who gave me plenty of attention.

Was he the storyteller?

Yes, and I was his baby. He was *the* storyteller, in every sense of the word. When he would tell a tale, he would begin with something like, "No granddaughter of mine would be foolish enough to let some wolf or something come take her stuff away, right?" And I'd say, "That's right, Papa." And then he'd go on to tell the story.

My grandfather couldn't read, but we never knew it. He cloaked it well. I thought it was the natural order of things for the child to read to the adult. He would say, "Baby, read to me what you learned at the schoolhouse today." And I would proceed to read. Here's this adult giving me all this attention, and I'm just stumbling through words, and he would just sit there and allow me to work it through. Of course, I didn't know he *had* to let me do it. But look at the strength and confidence he was giving me. I would say, "No, no, no. I'll work it out." And he'd say, "I know you can, Little Sister. You just keep on. I know you can. You just go right on." So he would hear these stories and he would redevelop them, or he would contradict them. He told Bible stories, too, and that's why I love to tell them as well.

So you were a reader as well as a writer?

I read everything. The Nashville Public Library wasn't segregated when I was growing up. It was always open to blacks, and that said something about the library to me: Here is a place where blacks are welcome, so it must be a wonderful place. I had a different feeling about it than I had about those institutions that locked us out. The library had sense enough to throw its doors open and invite us in, and I accepted the invitation. I was there every week to check out my three books, which was all we were allowed. As soon as I read those three, I would take them back and get three more. Fairy tales and myths were my favorites. Even today I love mythology. I feel that I can learn a lot about a people if I know their mythology.

What troubled me, though, was that I never saw myself in books. It was very difficult to find *me* in any of the books I was looking at—except nonfiction. So began my love of reading nonfiction for fun. That's why I fight so hard for it to be read for fun and not just for research, or an assignment, or a book report. Teachers need to model it, but they don't because *they* don't read it for fun; they don't have the mindset for it. It's fun to me because it was one of the few places where I could find images that reflected me.

What kinds of things did you find about black people in nonfiction?

I could find biographies of people like Mary McLeod Bethune. And the poetry of Langston Hughes was available. I would even pick up the encyclopedia and go through it and look for black people. That's how hungry I was to find what we had done, too. But I couldn't find anything in the juvenile novels. I combed the shelves looking for them and could not find them. What I did read shows up in what I ended up writing about.

That explains the nonfiction. What about the picture books?

The reason I wrote *Flossie, Mirandy,* and *Nettie Jo* is that I wanted black kids to see a book with a picture of a beautiful black child on it—be it male or female—and say, "Oh, there's me in a book." And feel good about it. I wanted to have a little girl who was sharp and smart, learning a little bit about her history and a little bit about our language. That's why I wrote those books.

We've talked about your growing up. What about your current family?

I'm the mother of three very beautiful sons. The oldest is Fred, Jr., who's writing now. He's a sports writer for St. Louis suburban journals. Then I have twins. Robert is at Tennessee State, where my husband and I went to school. He's in English. John graduated from Northwestern in June, 1991, with a degree in mechanical engineering. We're very proud of our sons. Then there's my husband of 26 years. He's the wind beneath my wings. Believe me, he's my best friend.

Let's talk about this wind beneath your wings. You do books together. Would you talk about how that works?

That's the question everybody asks. "How in the world do you work with your husband?" What they're really asking is, "Do you fight?" We do fight, but never about who's right and who's wrong. We usually try to figure out the best way to get across the point we want to make. Sometimes that means that we have to take out information because we're overloading. We have to make sure the information is documented and researched. We take great pride in the fact that we try to write as accurately as possible. We're going to make mistakes, but it won't be because of sloppiness. We try our best to document, to verify. That's Fred; that's the wind. He does the gathering of the information and I do the writing.

The first thing we do is outline the book. Do kids ever groan when we tell them that! We have to have done some prereading in order to do the outline, so we go to the library and do some preliminaries. Then we do a broad preliminary outline.

We work on a word processor. I'll type a draft, and Fred works over what I've done. He adds information. I run a hard copy and leave big blank spots. He reads it, and he may say, "This is not working. We need to move this to another chapter because it will flow better, and I'll find some more information to put in here." Then we read together. We read out loud; we tape, and I listen. We talk—all the time. A lot of people think we must be attached at the hip. But some days we don't see each other. He's out, or he's on the phone for hours at a time trying to track down information.

I don't enjoy research. It's fun when I get to go some place. When we were doing a Christmas book, it was fun to go into old houses and see their holiday decorations. But I don't like the nitty-gritty stuff. I don't like finding 14 different birthdates for the same person and having to figure out which one is accurate. Fred, with that engineering, left-brained mind of his, goes after every little thing. I'll say, "1872. That's close enough." But he'll find out it was November 13, 1872, at 2 o'clock in the morning. He'll even go search weather reports and tell me it was a cloudy day.

Documentation is what it's all about. People will not argue if you can find original sources for your material. We try at all costs to either quote from a person who's using primary source material or use primary sources ourselves. It's not an easy thing, but it's worth it.

We also depend a lot on the scholarly works that have been written by other people. What would I do without Lerone Bennett's book *Before the Mayflower?* It gives me jumping-off points. Or if I need to verify something quickly, I know Lerone has done it; it's accurate and accessible. I have to give him credit for his scholarly work and for the impact he has had upon our writing.

Flossie and the Fox was the book that brought you to the attention of a wide audience. Some people are now calling it a folktale. Where did it come from?

It came from my grandfather. He used to tell wonderful stories. That man could mesmerize us. But if I told it the way he had told it, it would not be publishable because it was so long and rambling. Her name was not Flossie; it was Pat. He always named his characters after me, or my sister, or my brother, which was wonderful, too, because we became a part of this magical world that he had created. In his story, Flossie encountered a bear, a wolf, a snake—all the evil creatures that children might encounter—and then a fox. But she did basically the same thing each time, and it would ramble on and on and on. So I developed Flossie from that. I wrote it first as an easy reader, and Flossie was a chicken. And it didn't work. Then one day I said, "I know what's wrong with this. I'm not telling this in the right voice." So, I had to step out of myself and step into my grandfather's head and hear and speak the story as though he were telling it to me. So it was like I was playing both parts. I had to be me, and I had to be him. My heart was already open to the story, but I had to *hear* it. Now his language was not mine. It was very difficult for me to say, "And what do a fox look like, 'cause I disremember ever seein' one." I had to play with that for several passages before I finally got into it, but once I got into it, I found it came very easily. So that's how Flossie came about. But it came on the heels of a lot of attempts. Anne Schwartz was an editor at Dial at the time. I had sent her a manuscript that was really not very good, but something she saw in it prompted her to write me and say, "This has potential." She encouraged me to keep writing. I had sent her other things before *Flossie,* but that was the one that hit. Anne's a wonderful editor. So is Fran Dyra at Childrens Press. They have the smarts to leave me alone and let us do what we do best. They're not frustrated writers who are trying to write their own manuscripts through us. A lot of editors are like that, but not mine. Nor Ann Reit, who's my editor at Scholastic. I have wonderful editors. I have to give them credit because they gave me the opportunity to write some exciting books.

Do you do storytelling?

All the time. That's another thing "I do." People often wonder if the storytelling came before the writing. It didn't. I studied at Webster

University with a wonderful storyteller named Lynn Rubright. She wows her audiences, as does Ruthhilde Kronberg, with whom I recently coauthored a storytelling book called *A Piece of the Wind* (Harper & Row, 1990). Ruthhilde and Lynn taught this course in storytelling and puppetry, and it was through them that I began to loosen up. I was a good story *reader*, but I was scared to death to stand up without the book and just go for it. They helped me to do that. Then I started to draw on Southern heritage and the Southern story, and that's when things kind of exploded for me.

What advice do you give to teachers who hesitate to read Flossie *aloud because they don't feel comfortable with the dialect?*

I must tell you this story. There was a teacher who told me she couldn't do Flossie because she was uncomfortable with the language. So I said, "Try it."

So indeed she did. And when I had occasion to be in her school, I did my BEST *Flossie and the Fox.* I had my fox and little eggs, and I charged right in and did my *Flossie* well. When it was over, she came up to me with an odd expression on her face and said, "I've got something to tell you. I don't want to hurt your feelings, but guess what?"

I said, "What?"

"When you finished doing *Flossie,* one of my students said, "Miss _____, she didn't do it right. She didn't do it the way you do."

Isn't that wonderful? It proves my point 100%. If the kids know and trust the teacher, they will accept what she gives them. If she goes to them with honesty and with love and appreciation of the story, they will pick that up from her, and they will love it because she has given it to them. But if the teacher is frightened or turned off by the story, she will transmit those feelings to the children as well.

Even though you are well known for your stories in dialect, most of your writing is in Standard English.

I write in both. Like Paul Laurence Dunbar, who could write " 'Lias! 'Lias! Bless de Lawd! Don' you know de day's erbroad?''; and then he could turn around and write, "I know why the caged bird sings, ah me . . . When he beats his bars and would be free." I hope that in the writing I do I can be as effective in Standard English as I am in dialect and as effective in dialect as I am in Standard English. Language is a tool, not a cage, and I refuse to be caged by language.

Language is wonderful. We can do much with it, and if we free our kids up to express themselves in many different ways, their school experiences with language will be so much more meaningful to them. They will not be inhibited about putting things on paper, or in their talking. Let them express joy and exuberance, the joy of living; and then when it's not there, we can clean it up—decide whether to write "I am" or "I be." And if "I be" fits the story better, leave it alone. When I'm choosing a word, I never choose the *right* word; I choose the *best* word, and the best word is not always Standard English. That's what we need to teach our children—to find the best way to express their thoughts.

From *The People Could Fly*

They say the people could fly. Say that long ago in Africa, some of the people knew magic. And they would walk up on the air like climbin up on a gate. And they flew like blackbirds over the fields. Black, shiny wings flappin against the blue up there.

Then, many of the people were captured for Slavery. The ones that could fly shed their wings. They couldn't take their wings across the water on the slave ships. Too crowded, don't you know.

The folks were full of misery, then. Got sick with the up and down of the sea. So they forgot about flyin when they could no longer breathe the sweet scent of Africa. Say the people who could fly kept their power, although they shed their wings. They kept their secret magic in the land of slavery. They looked the same as the other people from Africa who had been coming over, who had dark skin. Say you couldn't tell anymore one who could fly from one who couldn't.

—Virginia Hamilton

1986 WINNER

Hamilton, Virginia. *The People Could Fly: American Black Folktales.* Il. Leo and Diane Dillon. Knopf, 1985. 178 p.

The first comprehensive anthology of African American folklore selected and retold especially for children includes twenty-four exquisitely crafted, individually developed tales. Historical notes accompany each story and the compilation as a whole is arranged by four categories: trickster tales, tall tales, ghost and devil tales, and stories of liberation and freedom. Hamilton handles information about the Joel Chandler Harris texts with dignity, placing those versions of the traditional tales into a historical context. Her impressive use of black English from several distinct cultures also distinguishes this excellent collection of folktales.

HONOR

Hamilton, Virginia. *Junius Over Far.* Harper, 1985. 274 p.

Junius feels a strong connection between himself and his grandfather who has recently returned to his Caribbean island home. When his grandfather's letters are suddenly filled with obscure references to pirates and kidnapping, Junius convinces his father that they must rush to grandfather's aid. Shifting points of view give readers insights into the thoughts and feelings of both the teenager and his grandfather, stressing the strength of this intergenerational

African American family. Ms. Hamilton creates a rich ambiance with a lyrical use of language filled with Caribbean cadences and rhythms.

Walter, Mildred Pitts. *Trouble's Child.* Lothrop, 1985. 157 p.

Set on Blue Island, off the coast of Louisiana, *Trouble's Child* paints a picture of life both simple and complex on the island. The narration shares superstitions, customs, folklore, traditions, and the communal sorrow of an isolated people. Martha, the protagonist, who was born during a storm and is therefore a "trouble child," longs to go to the mainland to study. Her grandmother, Titay, island matriarch and revered midwife, expects Martha to remain on the island and learn from her the secrets of healing herbs and signs. While the folks on the island watch for Martha to bring out her quilting pattern, a signal that she is ready to marry, the stalwart young woman's life is changed. Harold Saunders, an "outsider" washed ashore during a storm, and Ms Boudreaux, her teacher, support Martha in her goal to go to school and study science so that she might more effectively help her people. This is an intriguing story, a mix of the old and new, with a satisfying ending. Walters uses the island dialect with sensitivity, consistency, and readability.

1985   WINNER

Myers, Walter Dean. *Motown and Didi: A Love Story.* Viking, 1984. 192 p.

In a story of love, violence, despair, and hope, Myers describes the unlikely courtship of a homeless young man and an ambitious young woman confronting Harlem's drug culture. Didi's dream of attending college, getting a good job, and saving her family from poverty is shattered when she comes home to find her brother Tony high on dope. Motown lives alone in a condemned, abandoned building. His only treasures are the books he is reading at the suggestion of the "professor"—his friend and mentor and the owner of the Spirit of Life bookshop. When Didi reports her brother's pusher to the police, the pusher orders that she be hurt. It is Motown who saves her from her attackers. Though she helps Motown find a small apartment, Didi resists the possibility of a romantic attachment because the quiet young man does not seem to fit her imagined future. And Motown's experiences with foster care have hardened him against needing anyone. The leisurely pace of their growing love sets the stage for the work's fast-moving conclusion. When Tony dies of an overdose, Didi begs Motown to kill the pusher who destroyed her brother. Had Motown killed the dealer, he would have destroyed his own life as well, but this near tragedy is averted.

As the Professor and Didi rush toward the impending confrontation between Motown and the dealer, Myers asks, "What was Harlem? A place, a name, a gaudy easel of colors." It is a place where drugs kill while the police take payoffs. It is a place where the city administration responds to urban decay by demolishing buildings, leaving empty lots where people dump their garbage, and then disguising the results with painted tin window covers to make it look as though abandoned buildings are still occupied. But it is also a place where Motown and Didi find one another.

The Professor tells Motown, "We're all in the tribe from the moment that we're named until the moment that the last memory of our deeds is gone. . . .

When you walk down the street and you see members of the tribe falling by the wayside, you are to understand that that's part of you falling over there." Myers has created a beautiful novel that raises the question of whether we as individuals and our nation as a society can recognize and respond to this implied challenge.

HONOR

Boyd, Candy Dawson. *Circle of Gold.* Apple/Scholastic, 1984. 124 p.

Mattie Benson is the central character in this school and family story. There is much more to the book than a recital of the trivial concerns of a group of sixth graders. In the endearing relationship between Mattie and her twin brother Matthew, the reader sees the two children trying to cope with the death of their father and the disintegration of family life when their mother cannot deal with the loss. In Mattie's friend, Toni, one sees the value of having a reliable and steadfast friend. In Angel, whose name is indeed a misnomer, and in Charlene one observes the unhappiness and trouble that can result from misplaced loyalties. Through this cast of characters the reader experiences a theft uncovered, a mother's rehabilitation through therapy, and Mattie's discovery of her own self-worth. The "circle of gold" at one level is the pin Mattie wins for her mother in an essay contest. The larger "circle of gold" is the one Mattie discovers when she is convinced of the place she has in her mother's heart.

The gentle writing, the spoken and unspoken lessons, and the development of several concepts of human relationships were highlights that the Coretta Scott King Award jury recognized in this talented writer's first novel.

Hamilton, Virginia. *A Little Love.* Philomel, 1984. 207 p.

Sheema has no memory of her parents: her mother died after Sheema's birth and her father disappeared soon afterwards. Her maternal grandparents have raised her with love and great caring, but as she nears graduation from the vocational high school, Sheema feels the need to seek out her father. Her knowledge that he's a sign painter who lives somewhere down South is enough to set her on a journey of exploration and discovery, so she and her boyfriend Forrest load up the station wagon and hit the road. An extraordinary story emanates from the characterization of an ordinary teenager searching for her identity, with the loving support of her friends and family.

1984 WINNER

Clifton, Lucille. *Everett Anderson's Goodbye.* Il. Ann Grifalconi. Holt, 1983. 32 p.

In *Everett Anderson's Goodbye,* Lucille Clifton has encompassed the magnitude of a death in a few gentle words of understanding and compassion. Clifton shares with very young readers the five stages of death, writing with a warmth and simplicity that transcends any lengthy conversations, serious discussion, or maudlin sentimentality. When his good father dies, Everett begs, promises, questions, and fasts while his mother quietly supports and lets him know she understands. Ann Grifalconi's expressive black-and-white sketches deepen the mood of this classic, with its memorable closing words:

Whatever happens when people die, love doesn't stop and neither will I.

A moving moment of complete silence filled the room at the Coretta Scott King breakfast when Barbara Rollock read this winning book in its entirety.

HONOR

Hamilton, Virginia. *The Magical Adventures of Pretty Pearl.* HarperCollins, 1983. 311 p.

When god child Pretty Pearl announces to her older brothers, John Henry and John de Conqueror, that she would like to try life as a mortal child, they warn her about those humans and their "winning ways" before they send her down from Mount Kenya to try life in the American South during the Reconstruction era. In the midst of a long journey through the South with a cast of characters from African and African American folklore, Pearl comes upon a clandestine self-supporting community of free blacks whose only link to the outside world is trade with Cherokee and Shawnee Indians. Living among them, Pearl discovers that her brothers were right—she is so drawn to the humans that she must eventually choose between her own immortal power and her newly emerging identity within a struggling mortal community. In a compelling African American odyssey that draws from myth, legend, and history, Hamilton brilliantly explores the relationship between mortal struggle and immortal dreams.

Haskins, James. *Lena Horne.* Coward-McCann, 1983. 160 p.

Throughout her successful career as an actress and singer, Lena Horne fought against stereotyping, segregation, and racism by refusing demeaning roles and by refusing to perform in clubs that treated African Americans unfairly. Her insistence on placing her strong principles over the call of fame and money sometimes cost her work and, in her early years in show business, often made her unpopular among both her peers and her audience. Haskins characterizes the highly visible entertainer as a tough, intelligent, and ambitious woman whose struggles for self-definition began in early childhood and continue through the present day.

Thomas, Joyce Carol. *Bright Shadow.* Avon, 1983. 125 p.

Although the writing style is simple, often poetic, the plot of this brief novel is complex. There is a sense of mysticism, and the spiritual with characters beset with strained family relationships, insane cruelty, and death. Abyssinia, called Abby for short, is a sensitive young woman in love with Carl Lee—much to her father's consternation. Many believe that she has the power to "see" things, which gives an aura of suspense to parts of the story. With a sense of relief the reader finds in the conclusion that after moments of high drama, Abby and Carl Lee will have a life together. *Bright Shadow* is a challenge to the imagination and to the reader's ability to move at times outside the real world.

Walter, Mildred Pitts. *Because We Are.* Lothrop, 1983. 192 p.

Emma Walsh, outstanding black student, is entangled in problems in the all-white school for which she was especially selected. She also found that she did not fit in when she returned to all-black Manning High. During her senior year Emma has to deal with ostracism by her peers, a confrontation with a white teacher who showed only contempt for the Manning students, rocky relationships with her divorced parents, and the usual boyfriend-girlfriend complexities.

Although some of the situations seem a little forced, and one would wish for more parental understanding, the intended audience can relate to many of the situations in this fast-moving story.

From *Sweet Whispers, Brother Rush*

The first time Teresa saw Brother was the way she would think of him ever after. Tree fell head over heels for him. It was love at first sight in a wild beating of her heart that took her breath. But it was a dark Friday three weeks later when it rained, hard and wicked, before she knew Brother Rush was a ghost.

—Virginia Hamilton

1983 WINNER

Hamilton, Virginia. *Sweet Whispers, Brother Rush.* Philomel, 1982. 215 p.

Because her mother's work takes her far from home, fourteen-year-old Tree is often left in charge of the household and caring for her brother, Dabney. She accepts the uncertainty in her life until the day she encounters the ghost of her uncle, Brother Rush, through whom she can go back in time to her early childhood. By reliving key events in the past, Tree begins to ask questions about some of the things left unsaid in her family, so that she can begin to understand herself in the broader context of her family's history. This outstanding time-fantasy deals with the complexity of human relationships, the strength of the African American family, and the importance of understanding and acknowledging one's roots.

HONOR

Lester, Julius. *This Strange New Feeling.* Dial, 1982. 149 p.

This Strange New Feeling is a collection of three well-honed stories, each filled with drama, suspense, danger, and the creative ingenuity of slaves in an endless quest for freedom. In the first tale, Lester's lyrical prose includes touches of humor tinged with bitterness as he deftly chronicles the story of Ras and Sally, who help others escape by hiding them in bales of tobacco and finally find their own freedom in a northern city.

There is a saddening poignancy in the account of Maria who, in "Where the Sun Lives," enjoyed a few years of freedom happily married to Forrest, a free man. Forrest dies suddenly and deeply in debt. Maria is "confiscated"

He knew that smile and the tremulous fluttering in the stomach that went with this strange new feeling of freedom.

This Strange New Feeling
—Julius Lester

along with other properties that legally can be used to satisfy the lender's claims. Readers are moved by the sense of dignity with which Maria approaches the auction block and through Lester's forceful prose realize that it is only Maria's *physical self* that will be enslaved. Her spirit will be forever free because she knows "where the sun lives."

"A Christmas Love Story" is a dramatic account of an enslaved couple who make a daring escape to Philadelphia when the wife poses as a young white gentleman traveling north to receive medical attention. "He" is accompanied by his very dark skinned servant, William. Tension mounts and danger lurks at every stop along the four day journey to freedom. The incident closes with Ellen and William Craft (the "couple") having to flee to England to escape the vengeance that was an integral part of President William Fillmore's Fugitive Slave Bill.

Lester includes research sources for each of the historically based events to which this master storyteller gives such stirring life.

1982 WINNER

Taylor, Mildred D. *Let the Circle Be Unbroken*. Dial, 1981. 394 p.

Continuing the story begun in *Song of the Trees* (1975) and *Roll of Thunder, Hear My Cry* (1976), Mildred D. Taylor creates a sequel of epic proportions as the Logans face the impact of a racist government policy that threatens their farm. They must draw on the mutual support and strength of the African American community to pull through in a time of crisis. As in previous volumes, protagonist Cassie's gradual maturation is reflected by her ever-enlarging world and ever-increasing understanding of the complexities of adulthood.

HONOR

Childress, Alice. *Rainbow Jordan*. Putnam/Coward, 1981. 123 p.

Women of four generations are portrayed as fourteen-year-old Rainbow attempts to find hope and promise in her life. Her mother was a child herself when she became a parent and is of little help to Rainbow. The mother's youth, inexperience, and lack of education led to an unstable relationship between mother and child. Instead, Rainbow's involvement with other women of differing social and economic classes helps her to find out who she is with respect to demands from a foster parent, a social worker, a boyfriend, and others. Characterizations are splendid and authentic language is used skillfully.

Hunter, Kristin. *Lou in the Limelight.* Scribner, 1981. 296 p.

Hunter's scathing chronicle of the music business is a sequel to her pioneering *Soul Brothers and Sister Lou.* The song "Lament for Jethro," about a friend killed in a police raid on Lou's brother's printing shop, has become a hit and Lou and the group have come to New York under the stewardship of their "manager," Marty Ross. Marty, determined to break up the solidarity of the group by promoting Lou at the expense of the boys, has them singing in garish, uncomfortable costumes and keeps them in virtual servitude as they live in debt while he manipulates their accounts. They have become "slaves in star-spangled costumes."

The reader recoils at their exploitation, especially when Marty gives the key to Lou's room to a well-connected friend who attempts to rape her. In Las Vegas, another member of the group, Frank, is given a line of credit to encourage his gambling, and all the young people are given cocaine and other drugs until Lou comes to realize that nothing they are being given is "free." Marty steals their copyrights by registering their songs in his own name, and the group is forced to work as an opening act for a white singer "with a pseudo-black style and enormous popularity—with white audiences." Then a promised movie deal brings the group instead to a pornographic film studio.

In the midst of their troubles, the group derives strength from Jethro's mother, "Aunt" Jerutha, who comes from home to care for them; from Ben Carroll, a U.S. attorney determined to expose whites in the music business who are taking advantage of black youth; from newly found friends who arrange for them to perform in African American communities in the South; and ultimately from the continuing love of family. And always there is the strength of the music:

> Blues was art and blues was therapy; it took gloomy situations and worked on them, turned them around and inside out and upside down until you could live with them and even laugh at them.

Their harrowing experiences do not break the young singers. Hunter uses their journey as an opportunity for self-exploration, an opportunity for Lou to begin to define herself as an African American.

Mebane, Mary E. *Mary: An Autobiography.* Viking, 1981. 242 p.

This painfully honest story of growing up in the rural South in the 1930s and 1940s chronicles the struggles of a determined and talented young woman who always felt like an outsider, even within her own family. Young Mary's distinctive personal story is set against the backdrop of the ordinary and familiar day-to-day life, meticulously detailed, of an African American community in rural North Carolina.

1981   WINNER

Poitier, Sidney. *This Life.* Knopf, 1980. 374 p.

This Life is a candid, outspoken autobiography of the noted actor and film star Sidney Poitier. In describing his life both in America and his native Bahamas, Poitier recounts events that evoke in the reader feelings of laughter, anger, disbelief, and respect. At the time of his birth, Poitier's parents had left

Cat Island in the Bahamas to try to make a better living. It was their hope to get back to Cat Island before Poitier's birth, but this man (who grew into a rather well-built person) was born prematurely and given little chance to survive. His fight for survival seems symbolic of Poitier's entire life.

The writer describes some of the many challenges he faced before gaining public notice. The reader has to laugh at Poitier's attempt to earn a living by parking cars after he had learned how to drive by watching what true valets did. Many an accident was the result. He writes of participating in the total destruction of a restaurant in the deep South when as members of the United States Army, some of whom happened to be African Americans, he and his comrades were refused service. He speaks of voice and speech training to try to rid him of his island accent. Poitier describes the labored, disappointment-filled steps from bit-part actor to Academy Award winner and the touch of emptiness he felt on that special-award night because at that time both of his beloved parents were dead.

The book includes his activities outside stage and screen, his marriages, his friendship and conflict with Harry Belafonte, and his work with the cause espoused by Martin Luther King Jr. *This Life* is an introspective study of a man who has lived widely and, although not always, well. For today's readers perhaps the most significant message is conveyed when Poitier speaks of the fault of many of today's parents (in this he includes himself) who give their children everything and take from them the survival skill of learning the responsibility of working for things both needed and wanted. *This Life* is a thoughtful yet well-paced study of one man's view of himself and the world around him.

HONOR

De Veaux, Alexis. *Don't Explain: A Song of Billie Holiday.* Harper, 1980. 151 p.

Alexis De Veaux's respect and admiration for the singer Billie Holiday reaches out from every page of this factual, poetically written biography. The author does not dismiss the erring ways of which the singer has been accused. Nor does she overlook the high-handed manner in which Holiday was treated by the law. The story tells of some happy days and some days of hope when her family migrated to Harlem, reaching for the "good life" in the North. As a fledgling blues singer, Holiday was likened to the late Bessie Smith; and the comparison seemed not to stop there as Holiday felt the sting of racism that allegedly led to Bessie Smith's death. De Veaux's descriptions of Holiday's bout with drugs and her mercurial career that ended with the singer strapped to a bed in a prison hospital is written with a haunting beauty that makes the Billie Holiday story a book to be remembered between anger for what might questionably be called justice and tears for talent too soon lost.

1980 WINNER

Myers, Walter Dean. *The Young Landlords.* Viking, 1979. 197 p.

When a group of Harlem teenagers complain to the landlord about the condition of a tenement apartment building on their block, he sells it to them for one dollar so that they can take responsibility for the repair and upkeep themselves. With a great deal of warmth and humor, Myers offers young readers an appealing story about a group of ordinary kids who find out first-hand that, although there are no easy solutions to tough problems, the first step toward making the world a better place to live is to work together.

HONOR

Gordy, Berry, Sr. *Movin' Up: Pop Gordy Tells His Story.* Introd. by Alex Haley. Harper, 1979. 144 p.

The father of the founder of Motown records tells his own life story, beginning with his childhood in Georgia, when his father always took him along on business transactions because he recognized the boy's shrewd mind for figures. Gordy's business skills sharpened as he grew older and continued working on the family farm. When the sale of timber stumps from his land netted him $2,600, Gordy wisely decided to travel north to Detroit to cash the check rather than to raise the suspicions of unscrupulous white neighbors. He soon sent for the rest of his family to join him up North, and within a few months he had saved enough money to open a grocery store. All eight of his children worked in the store, and each one grew to be successful. However, it was his seventh son, Berry Gordy Jr., who seemed to follow most closely in his father's footsteps when it came to business. A fascinating picture of a gentle, and remarkably humble, overachiever emerges from this extraordinary autobiography that reads like an oral history.

Greenfield, Eloise, and Lessie Jones Little. *Childtimes: A Three-Generation Memoir.* Harper, 1979. 175 p.

Three women—storytellers and writers, mothers and daughters—each speak in their own distinct voices to convey history in a personal way that is unique and memorable. Photographs from the family album combine with each woman's remembrances of her "childtimes" to produce an unforgettable personal glimpse into history. Pattie Frances Ridley Jones, born December 15, 1884, speaks through family stories as well as her own writings. She was close to the slave days and remembers her mother who worked as an unpaid maid for the family that had owned her grandmother before emancipation. Lessie Blanche Jones Little, born October 1, 1906, writes of her girlhood days and adolescence, followed by Eloise Glynn Little Greenfield's writings of North Carolina where she was born on May 17, 1929. Each voice speaks of home, family, chores, social events, and courtship. In a direct style, deceptively simple, each woman tells of the fears and hopes, poverty and hunger, love and pride, and laughter and music during her growing up years. The text draws no conclusions for children nor forces readers to study history, but this unique and vibrant compilation has an effect that is poignant and moving. The patterns of the telling link one child to the next and all to the reader. Few books have brought the everyday life of history to readers so vividly and effectively.

Haskins, James. *Andrew Young: Young Man with a Mission.* Il. with photographs. Lothrop, 1979. 192 p.

The son of an affluent dentist in New Orleans, Andrew Young was a precocious child who started kindergarten at age three and graduated from Howard University when he was just nineteen. He became an activist in the civil rights movement as a young minister in Thomasville, Georgia, and his talents as a diplomat and organizer soon thrust him into a leadership role within the Southern Christian Leadership Conference (SCLC). In 1972 he became the first African American congressman elected from the South since the Reconstruction era, and in 1976 he was appointed by President Jimmy Carter as the United States ambassador to the United Nations. In the arena of international politics, Ambassador Young became known for his directness and for his unwavering stand for human rights, a stance that was often critical of the U.S. power structure. This straightforward biography does not shy away from the controversy that surrounded Andrew Young in his public life.

Haskins, James. *James Van DerZee: The Picture Takin' Man.* Il. with Van DerZee photographs. Dodd, 1979. 252 p.

The work of James Van DerZee was unrecognized and virtually unknown in the art world until his photographs of Harlem in the 1920s and 1930s were featured in a 1968 exhibition at the Metropolitan Museum of Art entitled "Harlem on My Mind." At the time, the photographer was eighty-three years old. Because James Van DerZee's life spanned the twentieth century, because he had been able to document in photographs only a small part of what his trained eye had seen over the years, and because very little had been written about him for either adults or children, Haskins was determined to get the full story down in print by conducting interviews and corresponding with the man himself. This engaging account, based on those interviews, creates a portrait with words of the intelligent, hard-working, and dignified man who became known for his portraits of African Americans—men, women, and children of Harlem who shared these traits with the man behind the camera.

Southerland, Ellease. *Let the Lion Eat Straw.* Scribner, 1979. 247 p.

Abeba Williams spent her early years in the nurturing care of Mamma Habbleshaw in rural North Carolina. Abeba's tranquil life was changed when her natural mother took her to New York. Abeba is a strong, sensitive character who grows from childhood to womanhood under a variety of circumstances. She survives her mother's sometimes volatile temper, the advances of an incestuous uncle, and a marriage to a man who she later learns has a history of insanity. After raising a very large family and using her musical talent as a sustaining force, Abeba dies in peace, a well-respected woman in the community. *Let the Lion Eat Straw* is a moving story, written in rhythmic, poetic prose. It is the story of a truly genteel woman.

1979   WINNER

Davis, Ossie. *Escape to Freedom; A Play about Young Frederick Douglass.* Viking, 1978. 89 p.

Ossie Davis, playwright and actor, lends his artistic talent to the writing of a play that affords young readers a chance to reenact scenes from the life of abolitionist Frederick Douglass. The scenes are dramatic and forthright, withholding none of the vindictiveness of cruel slave masters, as if to forcefully demonstrate the reasons for Douglass's determination to escape to freedom. The play tells of Douglass's accomplishments as a lecturer, a newspaper editor, and a fighter for women's rights at a time when such a thing was basically unheard of. Douglass's fighting spirit is summed up in a speech made after he whipped his master in a "fair fight":

> I'm free . . . I know I'm still in bondage but I got a feeling—the most important feeling in the world—I'm free.

Freedom songs are interspersed among the scenes, and there are directions for staging. However, serious copyright limitations seemed to have been placed on the use of the script for "other than personal reading." But even in that context, this powerful minidrama is well worth reading and sharing.

Fenner, Carol. *The Skates of Uncle Richard.* Il. Ati Forberg. Random, 1978. 46 p.

The champion star skater who once fueled the dreams of nine-year-old Marsha disappears when the ice skates she'd hoped for at Christmas turn out to be ugly, old-fashioned hockey skates that once belonged to her Uncle Richard. But the dream skater gradually returns after Marsha gets an impromptu skating lesson—and a demonstration of some fancy footwork on the ice—from the former owner of the skates. For readers making the transition to books divided into chapters, this is an easy-to-read transition to this format—and a story that shows how hard work and determination are essential elements to make dreams come true.

Hamilton, Virginia. *Justice and Her Brothers.* Greenwillow, 1978. 217 p.

At first eleven-year-old Justice blames the pervasive sense of eeriness enveloping her home on the fact that it's the first summer she and her older brothers have been left on their own during the day while their dad is at work and their mom is enrolled in college classes. But gradually, she, her brothers, and their young neighbor, Dorian, begin to realize that the telepathic powers they all possess are greatly heightened when they work together as a unit. To their great surprise, they also realize that Justice is genetically predestined for greatness as their leader, a fact that doesn't sit well with her older brother Thomas. The compelling, original science fiction story is rooted in the reality of small-town family life, sibling rivalry, and a young girl's transformation from a fretting, uncertain child into a confident young woman ready to face whatever challenges the future may hold.

Patterson, Lillie. *Benjamin Banneker: Genius of Early America.* Il. David Scott Brown. Abington, 1978. 142 p.

Born on his family's tobacco farm in Maryland on November 9, 1731, Benjamin Banneker was taught to read by his grandmother, who came to the colonies as Molly Walsh, an English indentured servant. Banneker's grandfather, son of a tribal king in Senegal, and his father, a freed slave from Guinea, taught him to observe the world of plants and animals around him. In a school opened by a Quaker neighbor, Banneker learned literature, history, and mathematics.

Lillie Patterson details the impact Banneker's lifelong fascination with numbers and technology had on his neighbors and ultimately his country. He built the first clock made entirely from parts manufactured in the colonies; he calculated accurate almanacs to guide farmers, fishermen, and sailors; and, at Thomas Jefferson's suggestion, he was appointed by George Washington to help survey the new nation's capital. When Pierre L'Enfant walked out on the project and returned to France with his plans, it was Banneker's expertise and continued involvement that made possible the realization of those plans in the beautiful design of Washington, D. C.

Patterson not only makes clear that the striking beauty of the Washington, D.C., capital district is the product of this African American genius's dedication, but also she emphasizes the progressive foresight he had. Banneker's 1793 almanac outlined a plan for a U.S. Secretary of Peace to establish free schools throughout the country to work for world peace. A later almanac warned against the dangers of smoking.

Patterson gracefully combines facts with fictionalized conversations. She carefully distinguishes between fact and myth, providing enough information to dramatize history while suggesting that young readers go on to more-sophisticated accounts. Underlying both this biography and Banneker's life is the wisdom, learned from his grandmother, that "life is an adventure in learning."

Peterson, Jeanne Whitehouse. *I Have a Sister, My Sister Is Deaf.* Harper, 1977. unp.

In prose that has the rhythm of poetry, Jeanne Peterson has written a story that will speak to all who work with those who cannot hear. As a loving and patient sister, she tells the reader how a deaf person understands certain things such as the barking of a dog contrasted with the purring of a cat sitting in the person's lap. She makes note of things that bring fright to a hearing child but that do not bother the deaf child—such as a clap of thunder on a stormy night or the banging of a shutter when the wind is high. She talks of the companionship that is shared as the sisters walk through the woods: "I am the one who listens for small sounds. She is the one who watches for quick movements in the grass." The illustrations in this gentle explanatory book show a multiethnic group of children sharing in the experience of the one who has a sister who is deaf.

1978 WINNER

Greenfield, Eloise. *Africa Dream.* Il. Carole Byard. HarperCollins, 1977. unp.

At first glance, Byard's pencil sketches seem airy and dreamlike; but a closer look reveals subtle details that give a sense of reality to the far off African homeland to which a young child's imagination takes her. There is an impressive amount of historical information provided through the words and images. The illustrations of noble rulers of long ago, classic architecture, and graceful people make *Africa Dream* a book of visible pride and dignity.

HONOR

Faulkner, William J. *The Days when the Animals Talked: Black American Folktales and How They Came to Be.* Il. Troy Howell. Follett, 1977. 190 p.

Looking back on his childhood, the African American folklorist William Faulkner shares stories both real and imagined. Many of the tales derive from stories he had heard from a former slave, Simon Brown, who had come as a freed man to work for the Faulkner family. In part one, the reader encounters the hardships of slavery, the frustrating powerlessness of the men and women enslaved by masters who used these individuals as they pleased—in terms of work, sex, and aggression. These stories are told without rancor, but with the depth of feeling that stirs deep emotions in the reader.

In part two Faulkner turns his pen to a dignified telling of animal stories with important information given about the symbolic importance of Brer Rabbit and his companions. In an introduction to this section Faulkner states:

> Signs of unrest, dissatisfaction and even outright protest are easy to detect in some of the longer dramatic tales. As the animals behaved in the stories so the slaves were motivated to behave in their struggle to survive. Although weaponless and defenseless, the slaves, like the small animals could at times get the better of their powerful adversaries through cunning, careful planning and occasionally social action.

Faulkner's message blended with his marvelous storytelling style made him a natural choice for Coretta Scott King Award Honors.

Glass, Frankcina. *Marvin and Tige.* St. Martin's, 1977. 232 p.

Tige at age eleven is an illiterate African American street urchin on his own after the sudden death of his mother. He survives by his wit and his ability to steal and to "find" adequate shelter. Finally, this continuous fight for survival gets the best of him and he plans suicide. At that moment in steps Marvin, a down and out, once-upon-a-time successful business man. This unlikely interracial combination team up and begin to make life livable—two lonely people who have found solace in each other. In a little more than credible series of events, Marvin finds Tige's father who had abandoned Tige's mother before the child's birth. Marvin convinces Richard Davis that he must give his son a rightful place in his family. The bittersweet ending sees Tige established in his new home but with the ties to his friend Marvin still intact. This is a warm story with touches of humor, discussions about religious beliefs, and ideas about death and the value of education. It is the story of two people who cared about each other with a relationship unencumbered by racial differences.

Greenfield, Eloise. *Mary McLeod Bethune.* Crowell, 1977. 32 p.

This sympathetic portrayal of one of the great heroines in American history is simply told but never simplistic. Greenfield skillfully weaves into the personal history of Mary McLeod Bethune aspects of post-Civil War life in America and the trauma of segregation. This straightforward telling of Bethune's unflagging devotion to making the lives of black people better through education includes a brief introduction to some of the noted personalities with whom she worked to attain her goal—money for her educational projects. Particularly interesting is the discussion of her working relationship and warm friendship with Eleanor Roosevelt. Bethune's endless struggles to make her dreams come true are as impressive as her ability to bring African Americans together to solve problems long neglected by the establishment.

Haskins, James. *Barbara Jordan.* Il. with photographs. Dial, 1977. 215 p.

> When the Constitution of the United States was completed . . . I felt somehow that George Washington and Alexander Hamilton just left me out by mistake. But through the process of amendment, interpretation, and court decision I have finally been included in "We the people."

Former congresswoman from Texas, Barbara Jordan first came to national attention as a member of the House Judiciary Committee during the Watergate hearings in 1974. Her strongly held, eloquently expressed opinions have won her friends and enemies in political circles. James Haskins captures the complexity of Barbara Jordan and her times through the eyes of her supporters and her critics. Although this biography focuses on Jordan's life as a leading political figure in Washington, D. C., Haskins provides background information that helps readers acquire a full picture of her dynamic personality.

Barbara Jordan's eloquent speaking ability and decisive critical thinking skills were nurtured from early childhood by her maternal grandfather who encouraged her to be an independent thinker. She continued to be impressive as a speaker when she was on the debating team at Texas Southern University.

Jordan's political career was marked with defeat the first few times she sought office: 1962 when she ran for the Texas House of Representatives, and again in 1964. Jordan won her seat in the Texas House of Representatives in 1965, the first African American in the Texas House since 1883. Haskins describes Jordan's career as a member of the national House of Representatives (taking office in January 1973), her appointment to the powerful Judiciary Committee, and her influential discourse during the Watergate hearings.

Haskins has provided for young adult readers the life story of a woman whose firm belief in her country may be summed up in a statement she made at the 1976 Democratic convention:

> We cannot improve on the system of government handed down to us by the founders of the Republic, but we can find new ways to implement that system and realize our destiny.

Patterson, Lillie. *Coretta Scott King.* Garrard, 1977. 96 p.

This biography begins with the dilemma of the talented Coretta Scott of choosing between a musical career and the man she loves. She assumes the role of wife and mother during the years of the organized, nonviolent civil rights protests in the South. Beginning with the Montgomery bus boycott in 1955, when the threat of violence was nearly constant, Patterson recognizes the strength and stability Coretta Scott King brought to her family and their friends and acquaintances. The emphasis is on her self-sacrifice and dedication to family. The only time she raises her voice, writes Patterson, is after a sleepless night during which she receives 40 hate calls. The book imparts well the nonviolent attitude the Kings had to practice in their personal and private lives to stay focused on the larger goal of civil rights.

Stewart, Ruth Ann. *Portia: The Life of Portia Washington Pittman, The Daughter of Booker T. Washington.* Doubleday, 1977. 154 p.

Written with sensitive objectivity, this biography presents a clear picture of Portia Washington Pittman who lived a riches-to-almost-rags life with admirable dignity. From childhood she was aware of the stature and importance of her renowned father, Booker T. Washington; details of the famous educator's life are deftly woven into the Portia story. It is of great interest to note in this biography that in spite of Booker T. Washington's outspoken support of segregation, he sent his only daughter to northern schools and colleges where she was the only black allowed to enroll. As a young woman Portia traveled abroad to study piano under a German master musician. At the same time her father was getting financial support from wealthy white philanthropists who valued the concept on which Washington was founding Tuskegee Institute:

> Cast down your bucket where you are. . . . Cast it down in agriculture, mechanics, in commerce and domestic service and in the professions. We shall prosper as we learn to dignify and glorify common labor.

The biography recalls Portia Washington's meeting with her father's adversary, W. E. B. DuBois, dining with presidents, studying under George Washington Carver, her marriage to architect Sidney Pittman, and the birth and death of her three children. There is a frank discussion of the life and death of her favorite son, Booker, a talented musician who died a victim of drug addiction. In later life one reads of her struggle to save her father's birthplace as a historical site in Virginia.

The writer evokes a sense of melancholy as she describes Portia Pittman's slow decline into poverty following her dismissal from the faculty of Tuskegee Institute, seemingly politically motivated, her living in squalor in Washington, D. C., and finally dying at ninety in peace and dignity in a home provided for her by members of the Washington, D. C., Tuskegee Alumni Association. Well-selected black-and-white photographs give an added dimension to this well-written biography.

1977 WINNER

Haskins, James. *The Story of Stevie Wonder.* Il. with photographs. Lothrop, 1976. 126 p.

A powerful story of remarkable achievement emerges from this well-written biography of a popular singer, songwriter, and musician. Blind from birth, Steveland Morris was always encouraged by his family to explore and develop his other senses, especially his senses of touch and hearing. While he was still a toddler, his mother bought him a set of cardboard drums and a toy harmonica. Stevie's musical abilities became so well known around his community that friends and neighbors bought him a real drum set, a real harmonica, and, when he was seven years old, a second-hand piano. By the time he came to the attention of Motown a few years later, he was already an accomplished musician, and Motown called him "Little Stevie Wonder, the twelve-year-old genius." Haskins tells Stevie Wonder's story by tracing his personal as well as his musical accomplishments.

HONOR

Clifton, Lucille. *Everett Anderson's Friend.* Il. Ann Grifalconi. Holt, 1976. unp.

In a series of books, the voice of Everett Anderson has spoken to young readers through the words of a poet who understands childhood concerns. In "real boy" fashion, Everett Anderson takes a dislike to his neighbor, Maria. How could he like a girl who can beat him in racing and play ball better than he can! But when Everett Anderson loses his key and goes into Maria's apartment until his mother comes home—everything changes. Everett Anderson finds friendship in Apartment 3A—and even learns something about food from the Hispanic culture. With bouncy verse and quick poetic sketches, Clifton, a gifted storyteller, provides young readers not only with a joyful verse but, more importantly, with a "slice of life" experience worthy of being remembered. Ann Grifalconi's illustrations capture the warmth of the author's text.

Taylor, Mildred D. *Roll of Thunder, Hear My Cry.* Dial, 1976. 276 p.

Set in rural Mississippi during the depression, this novel chronicles the lives of a strong African American family struggling to hold on to their land, as seen through the eyes of their young daughter, Cassie. In spite of hard times, economically and socially, the extended Logan family fills its household with love, security, and dignity, creating and maintaining an environment from which all family members draw the strength they need to face the rigors of everyday life in the segregated South.

Blake, Clarence N., and Donald F. Martin. *Quiz Book on Black America.* Houghton, 1976. 206 p.

Based on scholarly research, the book contains probing questions about the achievements and contributions of black Americans in every aspect of American life. The format of the book allows the user to concentrate on an area of special interest or to browse through questions in various subject areas: education, business, sports, the arts, and social action. The book covers a broad time line with quizzes ranging from events in the mid-nineteenth century to the time of the book's publication, fulfilling its stated purpose to "make the acquisition of knowledge a pleasurable experience."

1976 WINNER

Bailey, Pearl. *Duey's Tale.* Harcourt, 1975. 59 p.

The music that was so much a part of Pearl Bailey is reflected in the poetic prose of *Duey's Tale.* In a mood of philosophical musings, Duey, a seedling from a maple tree, makes observations about life and about finding out who you really are and learns a great lesson about friendship. Duey as a seedling finds himself rudely stripped from his mother roots by a strong gust of wind. While bemoaning his loss of security, he finds adventure with a friendly log and a glass bottle. The three "companions" share pleasant moments together until the time comes for each to take its destined special place in the scheme of things—a place that is marked by change. A saddened but wiser and mature

Duey, now a sturdy maple tree, concludes that being different is not so bad, what really matters is that everyone "needs a little attention, and that's why people have family and friends."

Duey's Tale must surely have left the Coretta Scott King Award Jury with a warm feeling and a sense that the book, which might be called an allegory, would leave readers reflecting not only about the story but also about the author's philosophy of life.

HONOR

Graham, Shirley. *Julius K. Nyerere: Teacher of Africa.* Messner, 1975. 192 p.

A welcomed biography at the time of its publication, this book supports the view of President Nyerere as a dedicated, modest leader-teacher who worked to liberate Tanganyika and then Zanzibar and to join the two as the new country of Tanzania. Written for young people, the book lucidly explains Nyerere's political philosophy, which views society as an extended family and which incorporates both tradition and tribal pride into its political system. Graham's view of Nyerere is positive. The repressive policies and interparty disputes at work in Tanzania at the time are discussed, although interpreted to fit with the generally positive view of Nyerere. The author employs fictional dialogue successfully, and she incorporates excerpts from Nyerere's writings.

Greenfield, Eloise. *Paul Robeson.* Il. George Ford. Crowell, 1975. 33 p.

The story of Paul Robeson is offered here to young readers in easily accessible language. Greenfield smoothly compresses Robeson's personal story with his accomplishments as athlete, stage actor, and political activist. His developing political commitment and the repressive reaction against it is objectively presented in honest, unbiased terms. The timbre, style, and impact of Robeson's musical performances is conveyed. In addition, the effort and determination that it took for young Robeson to succeed as an athlete is told in terms that children can easily understand and relate to. This impressive man's unswerving dedication to pursuing justice and opposing oppression for black and poor people is offered with obvious respect, in clear and simple terms.

Myers, Walter Dean. *Fast Sam, Cool Clyde, and Stuff.* Viking, 1975. 190 p.

When Stuff was twelve and one-half years old, his family moved to 116th Street in Harlem. Six years later, he recounts his extraordinary first year with the friends he found there. Myers's first young adult novel is a tribute to the sustaining power of friendship as young people pledge to be there for one another and to understand and care for each other. "I just hope I'll always have people to care for like that and be close to," says Stuff, who seems to be speaking for the author when he adds that he would "like to be able to teach somebody else that feeling."

Myers is frank about the problems faced on 116th Street. The reader shares the pain of Clyde's father's death in an accident, the departure of Gloria's father, Charley's self-deceptive drug abuse, and the school system's failure to support Clyde's academic aspirations. The group's sense of community helps them face these challenges, as does Stuff's ability to find absurdity in adversity.

Myers's wit is expressed in his characters' language—their funny imagery and verbal sparring—and in his talent for expressing the humorous aspects of hurtful situations. When Binky's ear is bitten off during a fight, Clyde suggests a hospital visit to have it reattached. The doctor sees the frantic young people as threatening hoodlums, and the concerned friends are jailed and asked to roll up their sleeves to see if they are junkies. The reader will laugh at the almost slapstick farce, but beneath the farce we clearly see the intolerance that confronts Stuff's crowd. When they retrieve a handbag stolen by two thieves, they are assumed to have stolen the bag and again helping people is shown as futile even though shown humorously.

The closeness of the group is especially precious when contrasted with the difficulty of open communication. Stuff's father may finally hug him when he is standing by Stuff in the face of an unjustified drug arrest, but at other times his father finds it impossible to say how much he likes his son. "I guess it's hard," Stuff observes, "for people, some people anyway, to say things like that."

By the time Stuff comes to record these memories, the neighborhood has altered, the friends have dispersed. The book, then, is about a brief moment in Stuff's life, the world in which he lived, the community that helped him confront that world, and the universal need to find such a community in our own lives.

Taylor, Mildred D. *Song of the Trees.* Dial, 1975. 48 p.

Eight-year-old Cassie Logan loves the majestic old trees on her family's property almost as much as her daddy does. When two powerful white men scheme to cut down the trees for lumber, Mr. Logan comes up with a scheme of his own to foil the trespassers. Taylor's first published children's book shows the emergence of traits that would become the author's trademark in subsequent work: excellent characterizations, a strong sense of place, and the ability to weave a great story by drawing together threads of social history, the rural South, and African American family life.

1975 WINNER

Robinson, Dorothy. *The Legend of Africania.* Il. Herbert Temple. Johnson Publishing, 1974. unp.

The Legend of Africania is a multilevel tale. Africania is a beautiful maiden living in the harmony of her African homeland and beloved by Prince Uhuru. On a fateful day Africania is bewitched by the evil, pale-skinned Takata. She is taken to another land and imprisoned until she decides to become pale like Takata, to take on the pale-faced spirit's ways. Only when she learns that this imitation is the *real* prison does she become free and united with her lover, Prince Uhuru. On one level, this story is written with the flavor of the traditional folk tale. The Coretta Scott King Jury "read into it a much more significant story—almost an allegory. It is seen as a story of slavery, of resistance to a master's domination, and as a lesson in remembering to always take pride in one's blackness."

1974 **WINNER**

Mathis, Sharon Bell. *Ray Charles.* Il. George Ford. Crowell, 1973. 32 p.

This simplified biography gives young readers a glimpse into the life of a talented musician who, though blind, refused to see himself as disabled. The author highlights episodes from the childhood accident that caused the blindness to Ray Charles's special education, and, finally, his triumph as a performer of international fame. In this inspirational portrayal, Ray Charles is seen not as handicapped but as *handicapable.*

HONOR

Childress, Alice. *A Hero Ain't Nothin' but a Sandwich.* Coward-McCann, 1973. 169 p.

Benjie Johnson is thirteen and "ain't a chile no more." He is a junkie, and his habit is destroying his life and ripping apart his family. From Benjie's opening words of denial, Childress introduces the principal players in Benjie's tragic story. In alternating monologues, the reader follows Benjie's story from the perspective of his family, friends, and teachers. As the perspective shifts with each succeeding chapter, Childress weaves a tapestry of authentic voices, giving life to characters through their needs, words, and reflection in the words of others.

Drawing upon her theater background, Childress creates a novel that moves like a play—the spotlight shifting from character to character. Although the actors explain themselves to the reader, it is significant that they are not speaking to one another. One of the truths of this powerful work is the inability of the characters to communicate truthfully with each other or to see events from another's perspective. In one poignant moment, for instance, Benjie's mama wants to tell him that the "greatest thing in the world is to love someone and they love you too." Instead, this warm thought is verbalized with the mundane admonition for Benjie to brush the crumbs from his jacket!

Benjie's father has left, and his mother is ready to marry Butler Craig who lives with them. When Benjie, to support his habit, steals Butler's best clothes, Butler moves to a room downstairs. As Benjie's friend Jimmy-Lee Powell has said, "Needles divide guys," and the rift in Benjie's family seems irreparable. As Benjie flees across the roof of his building, however, Butler saves the boy from a near fall down an airshaft. Butler sees Benjie "swingin down over empty space, looking up at me, weighin' a ton and cryin' like crazy." Butler's tenuous hold on Benjie and the precipitous drop down the shaft become metaphors for their relationship and Benjie's life.

Benjie promises to report regularly to a detoxification program, and Butler will support him by meeting him there. But as the book ends, Butler is getting cold waiting for Benjie to arrive, not sure if Benjie can see him where he is standing, not sure if Benjie is late or not coming. The reader is left to interpret Butler's closing words:

> The wind is blowing colder now, but if I go in—he might get this far, then lose courage. Come on, Benjie, I believe in you. . . . It's nation time. . . . I'm waiting for you. . . .

Clifton, Lucille. *Don't You Remember?* Il. Evaline Ness. Dutton, 1973. unp.

A familiar theme is treated with warm family love in this gentle "lap" story. Desire Mary Tate is sure that her family can "never remember anything" because her father postpones taking her to the plant where he works as an engineer, her mother doesn't bring home the "black cake with the pink letters," and not one of her big brothers will give her the promised taste of coffee! Repeating her favorite phrase of total exasperation, "Dag, double dag," Tate retreats to her room and eventually to bed. What a surprise when the next morning—after sleeping late—Tate is awakened to find that not only will she go to the plant, but because it is her birthday, she will have the black cake with pink letters *and* coffee. In simple language that is not condescending, Clifton encompasses a young child's concerns. The book invites one to read it aloud to the many little ones who feel left out and who fear that grownups do not remember those things that are terribly important in young lives.

Crane, Louise. *Ms. Africa: Profiles of Modern African Women.* Lippincott, 1973. 159 p.

This collection of biographies pays tribute to women from various geographical regions of Africa who have made significant achievements in widely diverse fields. Some of the women cited may seem familiar to contemporary readers, such as the talented singer Miriam Makeba or the often imprisoned fighter against apartheid Minnie Mandela. Included is the intriguing story of a woman engineer, with one of the longest names imaginable—a combination of her father's name, her husband's name, and her feminine name, who was in charge of managing the water supply for all residents in Madagascar. Her knowledge and ability finally gained the respect of the men she supervised. Efua Sutherland, a writer and a teacher from Ghana, is recognized as a catalyst for having authentic African stories published in many languages. Sutherland became interested in writing for children when she observed the dearth of Ghanian literature written for young audiences. As a part of this interest she studied folklore and involved groups in the dramatization of stories based on the trickster, Ananse.

Lawyers, models, political activists, civil servants, and members of the medical profession are all a part of this book about women of color who achieved in spite of racial and political odds against them.

Hunter, Kristin. *Guests in the Promised Land.* Scribner, 1973. 296 p.

Hunter speaks in the voices of young men and women in the process of defining themselves and their relationship with an often-hostile society. The stories reflect the mixed hope, anger, and destructiveness of African American young people in confrontation with a racist world.

In "Hero's Return," Jody encounters his big brother Junior, home after eighteen months "in the house" for armed robbery. Where Jody expects to find a hero with improved "connections," he instead meets a brother determined to impress upon him that jail is not the romanticized retreat of street corner fantasies.

In the tragicomedy of "BeeGee's Ghost," Freddy must arrange for a proper funeral for his dog, whose ghost is haunting the family, because the pet cemetery would not accept "colored dogs." Having buried BeeGee in the backyard, Freddy wryly notes,

I'll never forget the night we spent with BeeGee's ghost in the kitchen. And I'll never stop wondering how some folks can hate other folks so much they'd take it out on a little dog. I bet if they knew it could come back and haunt them, though, they'd change.

In the title story "Guest in the Promised Land," Hunter's naive narrator assures us that "some people," like his friend Robert, "can't stand for anybody to be too nice to them." It was not Robert's fault that the trip arranged by white businessmen to the Cedarbrook Country Club did not work out. The young people were welcomed to play on the club grounds, but a sign on the door of the elegant dining room pointedly noted "Guests not allowed without members." When Robert entered to play the piano, his hands were snatched away from the keys while the "members" insincerely applauded his efforts. Robert expressed his bitter frustration by slashing the piano.

I . . . knew we'd never go back there unless we could eat in the clubhouse and listen to [Robert] play, wrong notes and all. Because it ain't no Promised Land at all if some people are always guests and others are always members.

Nagenda, John. *Mukasa.* Il. Charles Lilly. Macmillan, 1973. 120 p.

In this book, based on the author's life, Nagenda's autobiography tells of a young boy in Africa who realizes the joy and importance of an education. Mukasa was born to his parents late in life and became a protected "treasure" to his mother, much to his father's chagrin. When Mukasa's father would not help raise the money to send the boy to school, the boy's creative mother found a way to do it. Through Mukasa's eyes one learns something of the educational system in his village at the time of the story and of the ingenuity of the teacher who, lacking a great supply of commercial teaching materials, creatively provided students with effective homemade learning tools. In this simple setting one gains a little insight into the activities and pranks that are a part of just about every schoolchild's experience. One might accept as a major high point of the book the closing incident when upon Mukasa's return home after graduation, his father *asks* Mukasa to teach him how to read. It was then that Mukasa decides "Perhaps I won't be a doctor after all. Now I think I'll be a teacher."

1973 WINNER

Duckett, Alfred. *I Never Had It Made: The Autobiography of Jackie Robinson.* Putnam, 1972. 287 p.

With candor, Jackie Robinson describes the difficulties of being the first black to play in major league baseball—racially motivated problems, threats of physical violence from ball players on his and on opposing teams, and cruel criticism from several sports writers. Talent was not enough in a sport dominated by white players and white administrators.

Robinson does not try to gloss over personal problems that he and wife Rachel faced while trying to raise their children in the segregated South and in predominantly white areas in the North. The children seemingly suffered with identity problems—and for at least one—with tragic results.

In writing of his days after baseball, Robinson discusses the trials and tribulations of working in a management position for Chock-Full-O-Nuts. He also relates his attempts to work with the NAACP until what he calls "The Old Guard" forced his resignation. In conclusion this public hero explains the book's title, attesting that in spite of his success and triumphs, as a black man in a white world he *"never had it made."*

1972 WINNER

Fax, Elton. *17 Black Artists.* Dodd, 1971. 306 p.

Using as a catalyst a slogan he read in Africa, "Sweet Are the Uses of Adversity," Elton Fax researched the lives of seventeen African American artists who succeeded against the odds. In each life was the intimation that recognition in the world of art was difficult—and for a black artist to know success was even more of a challenge. As an artist himself, Fax knew firsthand of the struggle to reach the top. The biographical sketches not only paint a picture of the artists as people but each one provides a picture of the social climate in which the individual lived and worked. At one point Fax provides an interesting historical note about the early portrayal of black figures as clowns and buffoons:

> Since it was not common, prior to the 1800s for artists to portray black people with seriousness and dignity, few such portrayals exist. Race chauvinism veered white artists away from such a course, and the black artist, eager for commission, dared not risk offending his white clientele.

Fax pays tribute to an early twentieth-century artist, James Herring, who in spite of skeptics established an art department at Howard University in 1921. The author writes candidly about the controversy surrounding the noted sculptor Edmonia Lewis, accused of murdering two fellow students on the campus of Oberlin College, and of the tragic life of Charlotte Amevor who struggled as a single parent. Included is a chapter on Romare Bearden who, before his death in 1988, left a legacy of illustrations for young people in *A Visit to the Country* (Harper, 1989). One learns of the background of nationally known Jacob Lawrence, whose plates for *Harriet and the Promised Land* were recently recovered and the book reissued (Simon & Schuster 1993, 1968). And one is able to read of the dauntless courage of Faith Ringgold who was the 1992 winner of the Coretta Scott King Award for illustrations in her first children's book, *Tar Beach.*

The book is a valuable volume in the annals of African American history and even more important—a valuable study of the life and work of serious artists who happen to be black.

1971 WINNER

Rollins, Charlemae. *Black Troubadour: Langston Hughes.* Rand McNally, 1970. 143 p.

Langston Hughes's poetry and prose captured the rhythms of the blues and the richness of African American speech. He created art from the full range of black experience. Charlemae Rollins met Hughes when she was children's librarian at the George C. Hall branch of the Chicago Public Library. It was during that time that Hughes was writing and discussing poetry with members of the Illinois Writers Project. A mutual interest in quality literature and in the life and concerns of African Americans led Rollins and Hughes to strike up a friendship. This friendship resulted in Rollins writing this biography for young readers.

Rollins details Hughes's childhood, spent in many far-flung places. She writes of the loving influence of Hughes's maternal grandmother, contrasting this life with the troubled visits with his father who had settled in Mexico. The author recounts Hughes's experiences as he settled down in New York's Harlem, his disappointment in the large and impersonal classes at New York University, and the segregation at Columbia University. Eventually Hughes graduated from Lincoln University in Pennsylvania while continuing to call his "beloved Harlem" home.

Rollins includes details about Hughes's relationship with Mary McLeod Bethune, at whose suggestion the poet toured the South and where—through his poetry reading concerts—he was actually able to support himself and concentrate on his writing. Rollins points out how Hughes's seemingly simple language becomes a profound comment on the America he found in his travels:

> Where is the Jim Crow section
> On this merry-go-round,
> Mister, cause I want to ride?
> Down South where I come from
> White and colored
> Can't sit side by side.
> Down South on the train
> There's a Jim Crow car.
> On the bus we're put in the back—
> But there ain't no back
> To a merry-go-round!
> Where's the horse
> For a kid that's black?

Rollins describes in some detail the breadth of Hughes's work. In the poems she cites as illustrations one is struck by the large number of now-familiar images that have entered the vernacular from his creative pen. She describes the successes and discouragements of his life, his ultimate hope, and his death in 1967.

HONOR

Angelou, Maya. *I Know Why the Caged Bird Sings.* Random, 1969. 281 p.

In this moving autobiography Maya Angelou takes the reader into the innermost depth of her personal self. With a masterful use of poetic prose, Angelou invokes moments of laughter, anger, and tears and shouts of victory for justice triumphant. The story begins when Angelou, who at that time was called Marguerite, is a youngster in Stamps, Arkansas. Here she experiences the sting of racial prejudice and of family betrayal but also the support of her wise and compassionate brother, Bailey. With a respect for the older generation, she pays tribute to her Uncle Willie from whom she learned her multiplication tables as well as many survival lessons. Angelou's early life was full of knocks and hardships, but the reader is left with a sense of having been uplifted because the author leaves a message with young readers that with fortitude, they too can overcome. There is a significant note in the closing words. Angelou has a baby out of wedlock. A solicitous aunt insists that the frightened young mother take the child into the bed with her, despite Angelou's fear that she would roll over and smother the baby. In the morning, when she finds all is well, there is this statement of strength:

> See, you don't have to think about doing the right thing. If you're for the right thing, then you do it without thinking.

With *I Know Why the Caged Bird Sings,* Maya Angelou had done "the right thing" for the Coretta Scott King Award jury.

Chisholm, Shirley. *Unbought and Unbossed.* Houghton, 1970. 177 p.

In 1968, Shirley Chisholm became the first African American woman to be elected to the U.S. House of Representatives. She writes:

> In a just and free society, it would be foolish [to gain fame for these twin attributes rather than for one's accomplishments]. I hope if I am remembered it will finally be for what I have done, not for what I happen to be. And I hope that my having made it, the hard way, can be some kind of inspiration, particularly for women.

Written shortly after the 1968 election, this work is both an autobiography and political manifesto—an exploration of Chisholm's path to Congress and her analysis of the challenges the country must meet to become "just and free." She describes in some detail her early years with relatives in Barbados, away from her parents who were struggling with the depression in Brooklyn, where she was born. She was politicized as a student at Brooklyn College, an ostensibly progressive campus rife with racism and sexism. Entering Columbia University to earn a master's degree in early childhood education, she became active in local politics. She presents a lively portrait of clubhouse politics through the success of her Unity Democratic Club in establishing a stronghold for African American candidates and the tactics she used in the state assembly to create programs to assist disadvantaged youth in college. She also worked to establish unemployment insurance for domestic workers and to preserve tenure rights for teachers whose careers were interrupted by pregnancy. Despite her refusal to accept the "traditional politics of expediency and compromise," she was elected four years later to the Ninety-first Congress on a platform emphasizing jobs, job training, educational equity, adequate housing, enforcement of antidiscrimination laws, and support for day care —a program that would be no less relevant a quarter century later.

Having led her reader through the maze of Brooklyn politics to her landmark congressional election, Representative Chisholm proceeds to offer her analysis of the most-urgent national imperatives. Though written at a very different time in our nation's history, her angry, eloquent words remain disturbingly contemporary. She traces many of the problems to the schizophrenic birth of a country that paid eloquent tribute to "liberty and justice for all" while denying full citizen rights to African Americans and women. To heal the "breach between . . . promises and . . . performance," Chisholm argues that we need a Congress no longer controlled by seniority and cynicism; a society in which women's rights are a reality and "women of all classes and colors" have access to effective contraception and the right to choose safe, legal, affordable abortions; a united effort by blacks to assume political power; and real equality of education for all children regardless of race or income level.

> We must join together to insist that this nation deliver on the promise it made nearly 200 years ago. . . . I feel an incredible urgency that we must do it now. If time has not run out, it is surely ominously short.

Evans, Mari. *I Am a Black Woman.* Morrow, 1970. 95 p.

Mari Evans's striking collection of poems explores the personal and political dimensions of being an African American woman. The exquisitely crafted and shaped poems affirm the black woman's experiences of love, loneliness, pain, and "a black oneness, a black strength."

Using free verse and subtle rhymes, repetitive words and phrases, and evocative imagery, Evans explores the need for love and community. In tones of sadness, anger, defiance, and hope, she reaches for freedom from an oppressive society and from self-imposed constraints. She speaks of the need for reaching out for personal relationships. She applauds those who would seize collective power. And pervading all is her celebration of her African American identity.

Graham, Lorenz. *Every Man Heart Lay Down.* Il. Colleen Browning. Crowell, 1970. unp.

When he served as ambassador to Liberia, Graham was most impressed by the rhythmic speech of the natives of that country. Listening to this kind of patois French that seemed to roll off the tongue, Graham was inspired to write a group of biblical stories using this language. One product of this endeavor was *Every Man Heart Lay Down*—a story that tells of God's plan to destroy his now evil-filled world. It is the story of his little "picayune" begging to be allowed to come into the world and save the people, a simple telling of the Christmas story when worshippers from afar come bringing gifts. Graham included the traditional gold and oil from the wise men, but in keeping with the story's setting, the "country people brought new rice . . . and every man heart lay down." *Every Man Heart Lay Down* is a timeless story written with a kind of poetic beauty and simplicity that begs to be read aloud.

Jordan, June, and Terri Bush. *The Voice of the Children.* Holt, 1970. 101 p.

June Jordan writes,

> [Children] are the only ones always willing to make a start; they have no choice. Children are the ways the world begins again and

again. But in general, our children have no voice—that we will listen to. We force, we blank them into the bugle/bell regulated lineup of the Army/school, and we insist on silence.

To give the children a voice, the author June Jordan and then junior high school teacher Terri Bush organized a creative writing workshop in the Fort Green section of Brooklyn. The children came voluntarily on Saturdays to "rap, dance, snack, browse among the books lying around, and write their stories, poems, editorials, and jokes." Out of these sessions grew a weekly magazine, *The Voice of the Children;* poetry readings; broadcasts; wider publication—and this volume of prose and poetry by twenty-five African American and Puerto Rican young people, ages nine to fifteen, whose photographs accompany June Jordan's Afterward.

Michael Goode, age twelve, writes,

> Some people talk in the hall
> Some people talk in a drawl
> Some people talk, talk, talk, talk
> And never say anything at all.

But these young people have much to say about a world gone awry. They speak of loneliness, of anger, of pain, and of the ultimate futility of hate. Vanessa Howard, age thirteen, warns ominously of

> The last scream
> The last cry of pain
> The last tear
> Last bleeding face
> Last baby drops
> Last riot
> Last of the human race.

But we are offered alternative visions as well, as in "Drums of Freedom," by Glen Thompson, age thirteen:

> Some of us will die
> but the drums will beat.
> We may even lose but,
> but the drums will beat.
> They will beat loud and strong,
> and
>   on
>   and
>   on
> For we shall get what we want
> and the drums will beat.

Jerome Holland, age fifteen, tries to answer his own inner question in "Will I Make It?"

I clear my throat with a slight cough,
clear my eyes to see the way,
hold my shoulders up high trying to
forget the danger that might exist,
because I'm black and wanna make it.

Grossman, Barney, with Gladys Groom and the pupils of P.S. 150, the Bronx, New York. *Black Means . . .* Il. Charles Bible. Hill and Wang, 1970. 63 p.

Gladys Groom was the teacher and Barney Grossman the principal at P.S. 150, an elementary school in a predominantly African American and Puerto Rican neighborhood. The two adults were concerned by the many negative connotations they felt were commonly associated with blackness and began seeking positive images for their students—black, Puerto Rican, and white. They first encouraged a dialogue at home and at school with the goal of developing a "thesaurus of positive images." A close look at the student-generated products spawned the idea of putting the words in a book—a format that would reach a wider audience. The final product was the award winning *Black Means . . .*

Charles Bible's graphic drawings, strong positive black-and-white images, give dramatic visual power to this beautiful and meaningful book.

Peters, Margaret. *The Ebony Book of Black Achievement.* Johnson Publishing, 1970. 118 p.

As a high school teacher of English and American history, Peters was concerned about the dearth of information about African American history available to her students. She devoted her life to bringing information to the schools and to correcting distorted information. In this volume, she briefly sketches the lives of more than twenty black men and women from the fourteenth through the twentieth centuries who distinguished themselves as inventors, explorers, revolutionaries, educators, abolitionists, and business people, among other fields. Included are familiar names as well as others less frequently included in collective biographies, such as Granville Woods, whose air brake, induction telegraph, and third-rail system had a profound impact on American rail transportation. In brief sketches, Peters clearly presents her subjects' accomplishments, commitment, determination, and dedication to civilization.

Udry, Janice May. *Mary Jo's Grandmother.* Il. Eleanor Mill. Whitman, 1970. unp.

An early example of the cross-generation theme, Mary Jo visits her grandmother who lives in the country. The activities in which Mary Jo and her family participate are the gentle fun things that speak of unhurried and stress-free time—learning how to sew, playing with the animals on the farm, making goodies in the kitchen under Grandmother's careful guidance, and acting very responsible when Grandmother has an accident.

This book is one in a series of Mary Jo stories. It might be reasonable to surmise that the Coretta Scott King Award Jury selected it as an honor book to recognize a non-black author for her sensitive treatment of a character from a minority culture.

From *Let the Circle Be Unbroken*

The registrar's office was on the first floor. We stood silently before the door leading to it, reading the lettering and giving ourselves another moment to gather our courage. Mama looked around at each of us. "Ready?" she said. We nodded, and she opened the door.

A woman sitting at a typewriter, her fingers busy at the keys, glanced up as we entered, then back at the sheaf of papers from which she was typing. We stood before her, waiting. She finished a page, pulled it from the typewriter, and took the time to separate the carbons from the original before finally looking at us again. At last she deigned to speak. "What y'all want?" she asked.

Mrs. Lee Annie told her.

The woman looked as if she had just gone hard of hearing. "What?"

"Come to register so's I can vote," Mrs. Lee Annie repeated.

—Mildred D. Taylor

1970 WINNER

Patterson, Lillie. *Dr. Martin Luther King, Jr.: Man of Peace.* Il. with photographs. Garrard: 1969. 27 p.

A young reader's introduction to the life of Martin Luther King Jr. and his nonviolent approach to achieving racial equality. The simply stated information and the timeliness of the book, published just after King's assassination, were among the factors that made this book the first title to receive the Coretta Scott King Award.

The Illustrated Coretta Scott King Award

Plate 1. From *The Origin of Life on Earth: An African Creation Myth*,
1993 Winner, Kathleen Atkins Wilson

Plate 2. From *Under the Sunday Tree*, 1989 Honor, Mr. Amos Ferguson

Plate 3. From *Little Eight John*, 1993 Honor, Wil Clay

Plate 6. From *Brown Honey in Broomwheat Tea*, 1994 Honor, Floyd Cooper

Plate 7. From *Sukey and the Mermaid*, 1993 Honor, Brian Pinkney

Plate 8. From *Ray Charles*, 1974 Winner, George Ford

Plate 9.
From *Beat the Story Drum,*
Pum-Pum, 1981 winner,
Ashley Bryan

Plate 10. From *Black Child,* 1983 Winner, Peter Magubane

Plate 11. From *Aïda,* 1991 Winner, Leo Dillon and Diane Dillon

Plate 12. From *Mufaro's Beautiful Daughters*, 1988 Winner, John Steptoe

Plate 13. From *Mufaro's Beautiful Daughters*, 1988 Winner, John Steptoe

Plate 14. From *Tar Beach*, 1992 Winner, Faith Ringgold

Courtesy of the Solomon R. Guggenheim Museum, New York City

Plate 15. From *Nathaniel Talking*, 1990 Winner, Jan Spivey Gilchrist

Plate 16.   From *C.L.O.U.D.S.,* 1987 Honor, Pat Cummings

Plate 17.   From *The Talking Eggs,* 1990 Honor, Jerry Pinkney

Plate 18. From *Working Cotton*, 1993 Honor, Carole Byard

Plate 19.   From *Soul Looks Back in Wonder*, 1994 Winner, Tom Feelings

One ought everyday at least to hear a little song, read a good poem, see a fine picture

— Goethe

Illustrator Awards

Ashley Bryan
Carole Byard
Wil Clay
Floyd Cooper
Pat Cummings
Diane Dillon
Leo Dillon
Tom Feelings
Mr. Amos Ferguson
George Ford
Jan Spivey Gilchrist
JoeSam.
Peter Magubane
Brian Pinkney
Jerry Pinkney
James Ransome
Faith Ringgold
John Steptoe
Kathleen Atkins Wilson

1 9 9 4   WINNER

Feelings, Tom, comp. *Soul Looks Back in Wonder.* Il. **Tom Feelings.** Dial, 1993. unp.

For this book, noted African American poets were invited to contribute a selection from their works that best conveys the joy, beauty, and challenge of being African American. Tom Feelings illustrated the selections with striking copper-colored boys and girls—the youth for whom this book is designed to be an inspiration. Feelings captures the varying moods of the poems in paintings that give an individual personality to each piece. The predominant colors are the blended and textured blues, greens, and browns of Feelings's beloved Mother Africa. The illustrations of children, with beautiful dark faces, move and flow with the music of the poetry.

Using a variety of techniques and mixed media, such as collage, color crayon, and wallpaper, Feelings designed a book that is not only captivating to the eye but also musical to those who will listen.

Tom Feelings has included a biographical note on each of the poets who contributed a selection to this award-winning work.

HONOR

Thomas, Joyce Carol. *Brown Honey in Broomwheat Tea.* Il. **Floyd Cooper.** HarperCollins, 1993. unp.

The striking paintings of African Americans in *Brown Honey in Broomwheat Tea* give dramatic visualization to Joyce Carol Thomas's provocative poetry. Stirring examples of this visual feast can be seen in the strength and dignity of the white-haired elder's face when sipping broomwheat tea, in the artist's interpretation of the African American lineage as generations rise from the interwoven roots of a sturdy tree, and in the trusting face of the child who asks that "as you would cherish a thing of beauty, cherish me."

A touch of sunshine yellow illumines some part of each page—symbolic of the light of hope that is the strength of the African American race. Cooper's art reveals a sensitivity to Thomas's words, resulting in a book that in word and picture is a cause of celebration of African American life.

Mitchell, Margaree King. *Uncle Jed's Barbershop.* Il. **James Ransome.** Schuster, 1993. unp.

Set in the rural south, *Uncle Jed's Barbershop* is a story about holding fast to a dream in spite of seemingly overwhelming obstacles. Uncle Jed's goal in life was to own his own barbershop with four chairs, mirrors, sinks with running water, and a red-and-white barber pole on the outside. Beset by the depression, bank failures, and prejudice, Uncle Jed is forced to defer his dream. Finally, at age 79, he opens his barbershop to the delight of all who were his "customers" over the years.

James Ransome's paintings, full of vibrant colors, capture the moods and extend the text of Mitchell's story. Uncle Jed is a sturdy man, cheerful and undefeated. He is surrounded by a warm and smiling family. The homestead is a picture of care and neatness. One can observe the artist's care for historical accuracy in the paintings of the pot-bellied stove, the crystal-set radio, the oval rag rug—all a part of the era in which the story is set. Ransome's use of circular lines in the rotund bodies of many of the characters, the furniture, the oval mirrors in the barbershop, and even in the round aftershave tonic bottles on the shelf impart emotions of joy.

Ransome pays a tribute to his mentor, artist Jerry Pinkney, by including a character that resembles Pinkney among those in the picture of the people who cared about and supported Uncle Jed in his quest.

1993 WINNER

Anderson, David. *The Origin of Life on Earth. An African Creation Myth.* Il. **Kathleen Atkins Wilson.** Sights, 1991. unp.

The Origin of Life on Earth is a Yoruba legend of how the world began. Kathleen Wilson saw in the story a moving part of her own heritage. With breathtaking skill she translated the story into a visual "telling" through her distinctive style of portraying "silhouette expressions of portraits in black." As the Coretta Scott King Award Jury looked at each picture there was a sense of wonderment at how many details of the text were expanded in the illustrations. There was the care of detailing the stages in the molding of each figure, the quiet respect for the shapes of the disabled—representing orisha Obatala's moment of drunken weakness. And what a contrast between the distinctive and expressive features of the silhouetted story characters and the luminous clothing in which they are garbed. Wilson's unique artistic style gives unforgettable life to a well-told story that shouts her joy and pride in her African heritage.

HONOR

Williams, Sherley Anne. *Working Cotton.* Il. **Carole Byard.** Harcourt, 1992. unp.

Double-page spreads illustrated in acrylics with mottled hues set the mood in this powerful, visual rendition of a day in the life of a black migrant family. As the day unfolds through the voice and eyes of young Shelan, Byard depicts the strength of this family through large close-up images and lush colors. The beauty of the illustrations never softens the powerful images of work and struggle that are conveyed in the text. We see the immensity of the cotton fields and the strain of hard work, yet the tenderness of the expressions reminds us of the power of love and family as the summer heat heightens weariness. It is a celebration of strength in an unjust world that makes such strength necessary to survive.

Wahl, Jan. *Little Eight John.* Il. **Wil Clay.** Lodestar, 1992. unp.

Little Eight John, a familiar character in African American folklore, is an extremely handsome young fellow but just as naughty as he is good looking. Wil Clay has captured every nuance of this mischievous child's behavior in what seem like double-vision settings. When the text speaks of one of Eight John's tricks, causing his mother to have the hiccups, the illustration gives one the illusion of movement similar to sea-sickness! When admonished not to sit backwards in the chair, the chair suddenly becomes a horse, being whipped into frenzied action by this overactive boy. Wahl's adaptation of this popular story has a happy ending, which Clay captures in the affectionate scene between a relieved mother and a repentant Little Eight John. For a visual treat, the Coretta Scott King Award committee recommends that readers enjoy the fun of examining each picture for the details that tell so much more of the story.

San Souci, Robert. *Sukey and the Mermaid*. Il. **Brian Pinkney.** Four Winds, 1992. unp.

With his scratchboard technique, Brian Pinkney has captured many subtle nuances that give an added dimension to San Souci's interpretation of this tale from the folklore of South Carolina. Using gentle touches of color, Pinkney brings the figures to life in true character—the darkness of the evil father, the emerald sea colors of the mermaid, and the childlike pink in the clothing of the beleaguered young Sukey, who is abused by her greedy father. A closer look shows that the artist is also attentive to such tiny details as the part in Sukey's hair or the wisps of smoke from the father's pipe. The skillful blend of words and pictures assures the reader that *Sukey and the Mermaid* is a story to be read, to be told, and to be looked at over and over.

1992   WINNER

Ringgold, Faith. *Tar Beach*. Il. **Faith Ringgold.** Crown, 1991. unp.

Faith Ringgold is an artist. Faith Ringgold is a quilter. With her creative ingenuity, Ringgold weaves a wonderful story of hope, dreams, and dauntless courage "stitched" with the innocence of childhood. The reader meets Cassie Louise Lightfoot as she spends a hot summer evening on the roof of the apartment house—the city child's "tar beach." Looking at the sky, Cassie "flies" over a world in which her talented father will be able to work on tall buildings because, even though he is black, he will be able to join the union. She sees her family with enough income so that her hard-working mother will be able to sleep late some mornings. Then, with the mood swing that is a natural part of childhood, Cassie dreams of having ice cream for dessert *every night* because she will own the Ice Cream Factory. In all her "travels" she takes her little brother BeBe and all those who read this thoughtful picture book. The choice of colors and patterns for the material in the *Tar Beach* quilt and the arrangement of figures in the various scenes offer a three-dimensional feast for the eye and food for thought for the mind.

In addition to winning the Coretta Scott King Award, Faith Ringgold also received Caldecott honors for this, her first picture book.

HONOR

Bryan, Ashley. *All Night, All Day: A Child's First Book of African-American Spirituals*. Sel. and il. **Ashley Bryan.** Atheneum, 1991. 48 p.

More than once Ashley Bryan has voiced his concern that young African Americans and other youth are not being exposed to the melodic beauty and the historical significance of Negro spirituals. *All Night, All Day* is one of several books that this artist and scholar has designed to make the words and the music of the spirituals accessible and aesthetically pleasing to young audiences.

Bryan uses tints and shades of tempera colors to illustrate the changing moods of the twenty titles included in this collection. There is the bright yellow that glimmers in the abstract candles in "This Little Light of Mine"; swirling blues and sea greens wash around brown-hued feet in "Wade in the Water" and one cannot miss the joyous repetitious double-page spread design of the huge bells that accompany the spiritual, "Peter, Go Ring the Bells."

At the 1992 Coretta Scott King Award breakfast there was an unforgettable moment of absolute silence when for his acceptance "speech" for this honor book, Ashley Bryan played the title piece, "All Night, All Day" on his recorder. A book and an experience to be remembered many nights and many days.

Greenfield, Eloise. *Night on Neighborhood Street.* Il. **Jan Spivey Gilchrist.** Dial, 1991. unp.

Jan Spivey Gilchrist's use of warm shading together with blue, gold, and green colors clearly illustrate the characters portrayed in Eloise Greenfield's warm and delightful poetry. The expressions on the faces of the children and the adults and the subtle use of body language complement and enhance the author's beautiful and expressive poetry. The visual impact is further extended with the artist's use of silhouette and shadings of black and white. The passage of time plays a strong role in the book. Gilchrist's use of light and shadow to denote the time of day is impressive, and such details as curtains blowing as night approaches set a mood and enhance the overall effect of the work.

There is evidence of complete communication between writer and artist as one observes how the words and the pictures evoke visual images that change with each poem. The children's faces show adoration, mischievousness, apprehension, fear, sadness, and grief in the illustrations accompanying the poems. The adults, even when captured only in shadow or silhouette, convey movement and emotion. A fine example of this is the piece "In the Church." The interaction between children and adults is well presented in such pieces as "Goodnight Juma," "Fambly Time," and "The Seller." *Night on Neighborhood Street* is a magnificent creation of mystical appearances through the use of color, light, and shading.

1991 WINNER

Price, Leontyne, adapt. *Aïda.* Ils. **Leo Dillon and Diane Dillon.** Harcourt, 1990. unp.

Upon opening the pages of *Aïda*, one stands in the entrance of a mighty palace whose marble halls invite the viewer to participate in a breathtaking artistic experience. Leo and Diane Dillon, inspired by the voice of Leontyne Price singing the title role of Aïda, knew that the diva's adaptation of this tragic opera was a book they were meant to illustrate. Each bordered full-page illustration reveals some aspect of a palace of ancient Egypt, the powerful Egypt that existed as a seat of learning and a source of inspiration to the Greeks who followed in their wake. Although the lay person may not understand the artists' technical approach, the dedication to honesty in the portrayal of the characters, their clothing, and the setting in which they functioned and the grandeur of the period is clearly visible. One feels the texture of the robes. One senses the gigantic size of the temple gods and the strength of the supporting palace columns. The Dillons have taken care to give individuality to the faces of each of the characters in the panorama of people who are a part of this tragic drama. As if this were not enough, the Dillons' creativity extends to the friezes across the top of the page—a pageant of Egyptian personages that give visualization to the text. The depth of research in which the Dillons immersed themselves is a tribute to their concern with providing an accurate picture of the dignity and accuracy of an ancient and learned people. *Aïda* is the story of warring factors, a story of unrequited love and, finally, the fatal price of loyalty. *Aïda* is a book that will be opened over and over, and each time the viewer will enjoy a new artistic experience.

1990 WINNER

Greenfield, Eloise. *Nathaniel Talking*. Il. **Jan Spivey Gilchrist.** Black Butterfly Children's Press, 1988. unp.

Jan Spivey Gilchrist uses only black-and-white pencil sketches to portray a wide range of emotions—sadness, grief, joy, pensiveness—that are the themes of some of Eloise Greenfield's poems. In "My Daddy," Nathaniel's face shows us he is completely at one with his father's music and secure in his father's love for him. Nathaniel says, "He ain't never been on TV, but to me he's a big star." There is sadness in Nathaniel's face as he sits in his room, thinking about his mama who died last year. But one perceives a source of comfort in the shadowed figure of the father entering his son's room. Pictures in close harmony with the words demonstrate the artist's sensitivity as she depicts events in the life of the spunky Nathaniel and his friends. Gilchrist clearly understands all the nuances in Greenfield's poetry and interprets the poems with clarity and a warmness of spirit.

HONOR

San Souci, Robert D., reteller. *The Talking Eggs*. Il. **Jerry Pinkney.** Dial, 1989. unp.

A Creole folk tale from the U.S. southern oral tradition, *The Talking Eggs* features two sisters: a favored, spoiled, and lazy girl named Rose and a generous, kind, and hard-working girl named Blanche. The girls are given identical tasks by a mysterious woman in the woods, and Blanche is rewarded for her trust and obedience. This beautifully designed and printed version of a folk tale previously known to many in its Anglo-European variant features African American characters wonderfully realized by Jerry Pinkney. His drawing and painting show fresh observations of people and of the animal world. They embody a richness of detail and motion that is harmonious with the tale's idiom, time, and place.

Profile: Pat Cummings, Artist

RUDINE SIMS BISHOP

Cummings attended the annual convention of the American Library Association in San Francisco in June 1992, where we had the conversation that follows.

You've said you cannot remember a time when you didn't draw. When you were in grade school and high school, did your teachers nurture the artist in you?

I had a good experience with teachers for the most part. I remember a fifth-grade teacher in Okinawa. It wasn't so much that he encouraged us to draw, but he was an artist himself. That made a real impression. Art was something that was legitimate, something that people did even when they were adults.

Did you go to art school?

I went to Pratt Institute in Brooklyn, New York. At 18, I thought it would be interesting, even though my father warned me that New York *eats* eighteen-year-old girls. After living on army bases all my life, I didn't have a clue what civilian life was like. The first year I lived in the dorm. Then I dropped out, thinking I was going to join "the revolution." We had ten non-negotiable demands that we sat down to negotiate the minute they asked us to. We were trying to get black and Latino professors and a study center at Pratt. It was not well organized; it was just the mood of the times. This was the late '60s, around the time of the Kent State incident. After I dropped out, I worked in Boston for a year. My father kept introducing me as "my daughter, the drop-out," so I took the hint and went back to school at Spelman in Atlanta. I stayed a year at Spelman, long enough to realize that nobody knew that the art department existed. It was on the fifth floor of a building where the elevator stopped at four. I transferred to the Atlanta School of Art, which was a little like Pratt. For a year everybody there kept asking me why I had left Pratt, so I decided to go back to Pratt.

Painting was a way you entertained yourself as a child. Were you also a reader?

Oh, yes. Actually, my oldest sister was the one who read voraciously. I thought it was unbelievable that she could devour a book a day. I liked to read an awful lot, but not that intensely. I enjoyed fairy tales and fantasies.

I keep insisting that children, particularly minority children who have been excluded for so long, need to see themselves when they hold up the mirror of literature. Do you remember consciously seeking reflections of yourself in your books?

Language Arts 70 (Jan. 1993): 53–59.

No, and I don't think most children do. I think children respond to stories viscerally. When I was reading those fairy tales as a child, I identified with the princess. If the dragon was after her, I felt we were both in danger. Today when I visit all-white schools, I find that the children don't notice that the characters in my books are black until a teacher or librarian or parent points it out to them. The children relate to the content; they think it's a story about a boy and his younger sister, or the first day of school. On the other hand, I do think children might feel excluded if they don't see themselves represented in books. Seeing themselves offers a subtle reinforcement. They know they're part of the group.

What are your thoughts about this current push toward multiculturalism? Do you think it will be sustained?

It has to be. It's a logical and long overdue recognition of the way the world is. Now that we've entered that reality, I don't see how we can come back out. It's like trying to forget how to ride a bicycle. Some people are threatened by multiculturalism because they're insecure about what it means, but people who respect information and respect the truth realize that including a variety of cultures enhances the picture. Can you imagine living in a world where there was just scrambled eggs and bacon to eat every day? It wouldn't be very appealing. Not only is multiculturalism necessary, but it also has to be cultivated.

Even though the overall percentage is still small, there are a growing number of African American writers and artists. How do we nurture that and get more writers and artists from other parallel cultures?

This is an aside, but about five years ago I realized that I could call—at home—about 90 percent of all the black children's book writers and illustrators in the business. That's much too small a group.

When I go out and speak on multicultural panels all around the country, I keep seeing the same writers and artists over and over again. One of the questions that keeps coming from audiences is, "Where are the _____—the Korean illustrators, Filipino writers, Hispanic illustrators . . . ? So a group of us decided to get together to see what we can do. Initially, we called ourselves the Traveling Multiculturals since we always seemed to be on the road together, bumping into each other. One thing we started to talk about was finding and mentoring new talent.

For example, I met a Hispanic artist whose portfolio was informed by a Puerto Rican sensibility. I knew that one of my publishers needed an illustrator for a manuscript about a Puerto Rican folkloric character. I put this artist in touch with them, and he's going to do the book. His work will have something about it that a Chinese illustrator might not bring to it. Culturally, there are things that an artist can bring to the work.

The group that's come together is going to help identify and mentor writers and illustrators. Publishers are trying to do the right thing, and we hope to be able to facilitate their search for writers and artists from the various cultural groups. We don't want publishers to be able to say any longer that they can't find them. (Note: The newly formed group, called the Center for Multicultural Children's Literature, can be contacted through HarperCollins Children's Books.)

Do you think an African American manuscript has to be illustrated by an African American or a Puerto Rican manuscript by a Puerto Rican artist, and so on?

It has been my experience that if you write something from your own perspective, it will ring true. But I am not a person who feels that an African American manuscript has to be illustrated by an African American because then the reverse would have to be true as well, and it all becomes too restrictive. I illustrated Mary Stolz's book *Storm in the Night*. The story focuses on the relationship between a grandfather and his grandson. The author is white, but there was nothing in the text that said the characters had to be black or white or Chinese. As far as I know, she wanted the characters to be black. I feel that that was legitimate, just as I feel I can draw kimonos. I can draw something from all around the world. Artists can avail themselves of a virtual smorgasbord. It's important to find the best artist for a book, one who can really bring life to a manuscript.

Some writers and artists say, "I am a writer who just happens to be black." Then there are others who say, "I do this because I feel that black children need x, y, or z, and I feel a special responsibility to them." Do you fall into one of those categories?

I feel both ways. It's not one or the other. I want to do books with black characters from my own experience. I did not grow up in a black community *per se;* I grew up in the army, in a multicultural environment. I want to bring what I know to the stories because not only does that make it more personal and enjoyable, but it also shares with kids one way of seeing the world. When I was living in Okinawa, I remember seeing Buddha ash trays. Now you would never see an ashtray made out of Christ on the cross. That is a culturally offensive thing that only happened because people were not aware that the Buddha is somebody else's deity. In my books I want to share with kids some of what I've seen, growing up.

I also happened to have had a very happy childhood. I'm extremely close to my family, and I love them dearly. I feel very fortunate, but I don't think that all kids have a happy environment, and I'd like them to feel included in the one between the pages of my books.

Primarily, I do want the black kids who are out there, who have been underrepresented, to feel that they are represented in the books. I remember going to talk to a group in Portland, Oregon. There were all white kids, except one little black boy way in the back of the huge auditorium. When I walked in, he did a double take. He hadn't realized I was going to be black, and his eyes just lit up. He had felt all alone. I know it has an impact on kids to feel that they are different. It doesn't matter if it's color or whatever it is; kids don't like to feel that there's something odd about them or that they're different. They want to be included, and that's what I feel is the most important aspect of the books—that everybody feels successful.

Let's talk about your work. You said earlier that you had done magazines, free-lance work. Are you now doing books full time?

I'm doing books full time. It wasn't that I didn't enjoy free-lance work; I loved magazines and advertising. That's all I did. I really thought children's books were something you did on the side, for fun. The first editor I worked with took me into his office and explained that I should not try to make a living doing children's books. He showed me a map of the United States with pins all over it and said, "These are the bookstores that we deal with all over the country." He pointed to the South and said, "You can see there are very few bookstores down there." He was telling me black people don't read and that my books were not going to sell. That's how I interpreted it, so I thought you illustrated books for the art of it, and then you went back and did the real work. The real work for me was advertising, which is godless and soulless and heartless. It pays well. They buy your soul, but they pay you nicely for it. In my twenties, it was lovely. In my thirties, it was fun. And then I hit about thirty-five and started to think I didn't want to do that for the rest of my life.

How did you get into doing children's books?

I was coming home from one of the classes at Pratt carrying a huge portfolio, and a man in a car stopped me and asked if I was an artist. He told me he had a job for me at the Billy Holiday Theatre for Little Folk if I was interested. I actually went with him in his car, which is exactly what my mother warned me against doing in the big city. He did take me directly to the theatre, however, and I started doing children's theatre posters, which was a lot of fun. So my portfolio became full of art for children. I wanted to do children's books, but I had no idea how to go about it. At that time publishers would sit down with artists and give feedback on their work. I was getting a lot of feedback, but no manuscripts. I had also put a piece on the back page of the *Bulletin* of the Council on Interracial Books for Children, where they spotlighted photographers and artists. I received a call from a publisher who had seen that piece. Ironically, it was a publishing house I had visited previously with no success. The editor said they had a manuscript they wanted me to do. She didn't even ask to see the portfolio. I floated over there with my head in the clouds. She handed me a manuscript and asked if I knew what I was doing. I said, "Sure. No problem." Then I went home and called Tom Feelings for help because that's when I realized I didn't have a clue.

What book was that?

It's called *Good News*. It's by Eloise Greenfield.

What kinds of things do you do when you visit schools? Do you do workshops with the children?

I do presentations for the most part. I've done a few workshops, but they're not very productive because I have only about an hour, and that's not very much time. Basically what I want them to come away with is the sense that books are made by real people and that this is something they can grow up and do. It's a profession; it's not some inaccessible thing out there. That's how *Talking with Artists* came to be. I wanted them to see the kinds of drawings I did when I was little because that's accessible. I also want them to see the mistakes. I found they love to see how you messed up on a page. They want to hear that because that's what they can relate to. They do a drawing and they don't feel it's perfect, so they want to know how to get it just right. I also want to show them something about the process. I'll get the kids to volunteer ideas for a story, usually an animal story, and show them how that would get put together and how, as an illustrator, I would choose which scene is important to illustrate.

Talk about what happens once you receive a manuscript, someone else's text. What kinds of things do you look for? How does the process work for you?

The manuscript is offered to me, and generally I decide whether I'm going to take it, based on whether or not it's going to be fun to draw. Or else it's just a story that I love, period. What happens is the same thing that happens when anybody reads a text without pictures. I start to envision scenes in my head. Based on my first feeling about what might be fun to draw, I start blocking it out. I also have to take into account how many pages there are, where the pages are going to turn, things like that. I will mathematically divide the story up by 27 pages because most picture books are 32 pages, and you lose about 5 for all the front matter. So I divide the total number of lines by 27, and that gives me a rough sense of how many lines might appear on a page if it were broken down that way. Then I start pacing through and figuring out what scenes I want to pull out. I tend to like the ones that have some tension in them or action—something dynamic needs to be happening.

Your pictures are full of action—and humor.

You should see the ones that don't get published. There's one with the cat flipping in *Clean Your Room, Harvey Moon.* I had the cat upside down with his tongue hanging out of his mouth. I loved it. My editor has a different relationship with her cat than I have with mine.

What determines your medium?

It just suggests itself. I'm getting ready to work on a Spanish fairy tale, and I want it to be in oil because I want it to be lush. It's called *The Blue Lake.*

This is my new theory, my new concept: I want to live inside the book. I want to be there, to direct it more. When I did *Talking with Artists,* I noticed a pattern. Most of us illustrators are thrilled and excited when we get our first book. With the second, we're delighted to have the chance to do it again. By the third or fourth, we start to make commitments to books that may not really excite us, but we're thrilled to be working in the business. Eventually, we find we have five or six contracts, which could be three or four years of commitments, and for a while that feels like job security. Then one day it feels like pressure, almost like being an indentured servant. By the time we get to those last books, our feelings about them may have changed.

Based on that, I'm starting to feel that I want each book to be more personal. This Spanish fairy tale came from Augusta Baker. I heard her tell a story and asked her about doing a picture book. She referred me to some collections she had done, and I selected one of the stories. It's set in Spain, and my editor and I thought that Moorish Spain would be ideal. So my husband and my mother and I went to Spain and walked around in castles because castles figure heavily in the story. I really want to smell the environment, and taste the environment, and get into the culture a little bit more, and live within the book. Each book is something of a capsule.

Ideally, I want to record what captures my interest. For example, I'm really interested in Bali—the art and fabrics and things like that. I'm thinking that instead of just investigating what I'm interested in anyway, I can record it, make it a story, and share it with somebody else.

I've noticed that a lot of artists move from illustrating other people's texts to being both artist and writer. Is this part of that process you're describing?

Yes. You realize that nobody is going to write the story you feel like illustrating. If there's an image playing itself in your head, you may as well write the story that goes with it because otherwise you might be waiting indefinitely.

Who or what are some of the important influences on your work?

I think the fairy tales in my upbringing influenced me a lot. Fantasy has always appealed to me so strongly that sometimes, even if the story doesn't call for fantasy, I'll put it in. I like aerial views, because I have flying dreams. As I've gotten older, I've gotten more practical in my dreams, so that I even convince myself I can fly. Then I wake up. It's so bitterly disappointing that I find if I draw aerial views, it brings me back to that sensation.

Then there are other artists. I think my first book looked like a tribute to Tom Feelings. Work by other artists, like the ones in *Talking with Artists,* could immobilize me with awe, but I try to let it inspire me. I look at other people's work all the time. There will be some element, maybe the combination of colors or the way they use shadow or something like that, that will strike me.

Are most of those influences unconscious, then? There are people whose work you like, and some element they use just appears in your work?

I think some are surprisingly conscious. If there's someone whose palette I like, I might clip out something and put it on my drawing table. Perhaps I like the way they had brown next to olive next to red or something like that. Or it could be their use of line in a particular piece. I might surround my desk with things like that, but it's not a literal lift.

On to the future. At the exhibits I saw an advance copy of your new book, Petey Moroni's Camp Runamok Diary. *Where did that idea come from?*

A girlfriend of mine went camping, and she told me that while she was asleep, raccoons got her Cheese Doodles and Ring Ding Juniors. I don't go camping, so I thought that raccoons were out there eating nuts and berries. I thought she had to be kidding, but when I ran across another reference to raccoons stealing food, *Petey Moroni's Camp Runamok Diary* just came to me. I liked the title, so I thought maybe I'd do a story with a raccoon loose at camp to go with the name. One thing I liked about Petey Moroni is he's got this Italian last name. People might not expect him to be black, but I've got black friends whose last names are Cohen or Giovanni. It's presumptuous to assume that all blacks have had a southern upbringing or a ghetto upbringing. Those stereotypes don't apply. What I also liked about this camp was the possibility for it to be totally multicultural. I like, too, that Petey's the recorder; he's the one with the overview.

What else is coming up?

In addition to *The Blue Lake,* I'm working on a book about carousels. I like the way carousels look. Then, because I'm going to Ghana in the fall, and I've never done an African folk tale, I want to do a Ghanaian folk tale. I've also got a manuscript coming up from Nikki Grimes, and I love it. It's an alphabet book, a poem. It will be my first alphabet book, and it excites me no end. I have a lot of projects in different stages.

Any advice to teachers about nurturing young artists?

One thing. It's not a criticism because I think it's a natural tendency. I grew up with art teachers who would put an apple on a table and then have everybody draw the apple. It becomes evident very quickly who is the "class artist" because his or her apple looks most like the apple on the table. That effectively destroys a whole room full of potential. In every school I go to, everybody knows who the class artist is, and I wonder what that means. For example, I visited a school, and after my presentation the principal took me down the hall to show me a display of masks that the children had done. They were fantastic papier mache masks made by second and third graders. I wanted to buy them and put them on the wall at home. The children were lined up in the hall for lunch, and I was trying to make a point of pausing at all of the masks. But the principal was saying, "Don't look at those, come down here." She wanted to show me the one that was the most realistic, that looked most like a face. She had bypassed all the colorful ones, the ones with the imaginative shapes and the unique textures. The kids were conscious that all those had been passed over, and that unless their work was photographic, it wasn't being considered art.

But look at some of the styles that are in books now. Picture books are a haven for artists because they can use practically any kind of style, and children are open to it. So what I would say to teachers is just to inform themselves that art is more than their definition might be. Let kids have some free loose running space, and try to encourage the ones who want to stick to it. A child can be complimented on her use of color, or her use of texture, or on her imagination. Expose them to different materials and sit back. Art is not the sort of thing that necessarily gets taught; it gets indulged.

---

1 9 8 9   **WINNER**

McKissack, Patricia C. *Mirandy and Brother Wind.* Il. **Jerry Pinkney.** Knopf, 1988. unp.

Mirandy overlooks her obvious partner for her first cakewalk after she brags that she will be accompanied by the wind himself and sets out to catch her partner. The engaging full-color paintings are filled with historical details of African American life in the rural South at the turn of the century. They perfectly interpret and enhance the light-hearted exuberance inherent in the story and memorably characterize the pride, self-confidence, and determination of Mirandy.

HONOR

Stolz, Mary. *Storm in the Night.* Il. **Pat Cummings.** HarperCollins, 1988. unp.

Grandfather's lively recollections about his own childhood fear of a thunderstorm occupies young Thomas's attention during an electrical power failure and helps the boy overcome his worries. A visual story-within-a-story assists readers with the flashbacks. Cummings's ability to challenge the eye with color and perspective is as effective as her poignant portrayal of the African American grandfather and grandson inside their cozy single-family home on a rainy summer night.

Greenfield, Eloise. *Under the Sunday Tree.* Il. **Mr. Amos Ferguson.** Harper, 1988. 40 p.

Twenty exquisite paintings introduce children to the artwork of the Bahamian artist, Mr. Amos Ferguson. The playfully vivid paintings, which boldly depict aspects of life in the Bahamas, have great child appeal. Poet Eloise Greenfield has written poems to accompany every painting, further extending each painting's mood and meaning.

1988 **WINNER**

Steptoe, John. *Mufaro's Beautiful Daughters: An African Tale.* Il. **John Steptoe.** Lothrop, 1987. unp.

Two beautiful sisters—one vain, the other kind—compete for the king's attention when he announces he is looking for a wife. Brilliant full-color paintings illustrate the classic tale of just rewards. The artist skillfully uses light and color to give emotional power to illustrations that richly detail the natural beauty of a specific region in Zimbabwe.

HONOR

Langstaff, John, comp. *What a Morning! The Christmas Story in Black Spirituals.* Il. **Ashley Bryan.** Margaret K. McElderry/Macmillan, 1987. unp.

The Christmas story is told through a chronological arrangement of five African American spirituals, lavishly illustrated by brilliant tempera paintings. Brief biblical quotes accompanying each of the spirituals provide a religious context, while Bryan's shining iconographic portraits of a black Nativity provide a historical, geographical, and emotional context.

Rohmer, Harriet, Octavio Chow, and Morris Vidaure. *The Invisible Hunters: A Legend from the Miskito Indians of Nicaragua. Los Cazadores Invisibles: Una Leyenda de los Indios Miskitos de Nicaragua.* Il. **JoeSam.** Children's Book Press, 1987. 32 p.

An early Central American legend tells of the ultimate price of greed as well as the tragedy of deceiving one's own people. Themes concerning colonialism are developed in colorful, unique paper constructions and collages.

1 9 8 7 **WINNER**

Dragonwagon, Crescent. *Half a Moon and One Whole Star.* Il. **Jerry Pinkney.**
Macmillan, 1986. unp.

Half a Moon and One Whole Star is a lullaby that invites the reader to
share in the safety of untroubled sleep. It is the song of man and of creature and
their different activities as the sun goes down. It is as if Pinkney was an unseen
observer in the actions of each character in this gentle story. One sees the
brightly colored parrots "rest in jungles deep." And at the same time Pinkney
takes you with him to see "Johnny with his saxophone" standing against an
early night sky, Johnny who will play at the club at night. And while the
activities are either stopping or starting, with mood-setting colors the illustrator introduces you to the child who at the end of the day is lulled to untroubled
sleep. In a blend of words and pictures the reader, too, can sing of the night
that is marked with *Half a Moon and One Whole Star.*

HONOR

Bryan, Ashley. *Lion and the Ostrich Chicks and Other African Folk Tales.* Il.
Ashley Bryan. Atheneum, 1986. 87 p.

Using his special talent for blending rhythmic word patterns with all the
details of a well-told story, Bryan has adapted a diverse collection of African
tales that beg to be read aloud. Through his research into the history and
culture of several tribes, this author/illustrator found the roots of the stories in
many geographical regions and in his inimitable writing style retold the tales for
young readers. As the complete scholar that he is, Bryan included a bibliography, listing the source of each of the stories in the book.

One cannot miss the folk tale concept of the triumph of good over evil
whether it is the title story, in which the lion tries to claim the ostrich chicks
as his own, or a telling of how the born-foolish boy outwits the trickster
Ananse.

Bryan extends the text with his own art prints in sharp black-and-white
figures or illustrations using the earth colors of the land in which these tales are
set. The Coretta Scott King Award Jury enjoyed both the humor and the
"lessons" in *The Lion and the Ostrich Chicks.*

Cummings, Pat. *C.L.O.U.D.S.* Il. **Pat Cummings.** Lothrop, 1986. unp.

In a flight of fancy Cummings lets readers share in an imaginary trip to an
artist's studio where the painter hopes to see exciting new colors spring from
his palette. Chuku is a painter for *Creative Lights Opticals* and *Unusual Designs* in the *Sky.* His excitement about a new assignment fades when he is sent
to paint the sky over New York City and to produce rigid and realistic interpretations. But his creativity was not to be thwarted. Each day he draws sky
pictures in unusual colors and intriguing cloud shapes. There are Lovely Light
Lavender sunsets, Cloud-Lining Silver and Unbelievingly Brilliant Gold! The
cloud shapes take the form of tigers, giraffes, and birds, all of which were done
especially for a little girl, Chrissy, the only one in New York who ever seemed
to look *up.*

But all readers who see Chuku's figures in *C.L.O.U.D.S.* will find themselves looking for colorful skies in New York and elsewhere. They may even
look for a real Chuku who is a very purple young man.

1 9 8 6 **WINNER**

Flournoy, Valerie. *The Patchwork Quilt*. Il. **Jerry Pinkney.** Dial, 1985. unp.

The Patchwork Quilt is a story of family unity. In this story parents care, children are loved, and a grandmother is a loving and integral part of the household. Each member of the family contributes a memorable piece of clothing to the patchwork quilt, which symbolically bonds the family. Jerry Pinkney saw all these elements in the text and gave his personal artistic interpretation to the story and its characters. In the colorful quilt one sees a variety of textures, shapes, and forms. This same concept extends itself to the characterization of the family members. Pinkney captures the nuances of skin color, the individual hair styles, and the personal choice of dress. This care for making each one an individual speaks to the artist's philosophy of making sure those who see his art realize that the beauty of the African American is as varied as the people who make up this culture. The artwork in *The Patchwork Quilt* invites readers to visit a cross-generational African American family living in harmony in a home that celebrates togetherness.

HONOR

Hamilton, Virginia. *The People Could Fly: American Black Folktales*. Ils. **Leo Dillon and Diane Dillon.** Knopf, 1985. 178 p.

Forty stunning, stylized black-and-white illustrations accompany Virginia Hamilton's retellings of African American folk tales, echoing the dignity of the text by extending each tale's distinctive mood. The harmony of all book-design elements provides a handsome presentation of stories for families to share, scholars to study, and individuals of all ages and backgrounds to enjoy.

1 9 8 4 **WINNER**

Walter, Mildred Pitts. *My Mama Needs Me*. Il. **Pat Cummings.** Lothrop, 1983. unp.

Walter's simple text describes a universal dilemma—the concern and discomfort of the older child when a new baby comes home—and Cummings gives visual interpretation to the concept. She chooses mainly mocha brown for the family figures while the use of other colors gives the story a multicultural setting, thus extending the universality of the concept. For some observers an outstanding feature of the illustrations can be seen in the expressive eyes of the troubled Jason—eyes that show the perplexity of wanting to be needed yet seeming to be rejected. There is a visual sense of family, of love and tenderness, when Jason shares the mother's nursing moments and learns to "rub the baby's ear" to make it want to suckle more and when he is asked to help bathe the baby. From a sense of being an outsider to the assurance that his Mama needs him—Cummings's bright colors and decorative designs have captured the joy of this family story.

1 9 8 3 **WINNER**

Magubane, Peter. *Black Child*. Photo. **Peter Magubane.** Knopf, 1982. 102 p.

A stream of emotions ran through the Jury—surprise, horror, excitement, distress, anger, and occasionally a sense of hope. It was the Coretta Scott King Jury together examining Peter Magubane's *Black Child*.

Taking advantage of the sharp contrasts that are best captured in black-and-white photography, photojournalist Magubane has shown the disparate world of South Africa through the eyes of its black children. The pictures tell stories of deplorable working conditions where teenagers who should be enjoying life were sweating in the maize fields of Delmas and who return at day's end to windowless dormitories for restless sleep. One wondered about the future of the skinny-legged barefoot boy begging a few coins from a well-dressed white woman on a street in Johannesburg. As a tribute to the human spirit, Magubane photographed a youth making joyful music on a homemade guitar. The book closes with a dramatic picture of the grave of Hector Peterson—the thirteen-year-old who was the first to die in the Soweto riots.

There seems to be a special message in the selection of solid black end papers with which this powerful photo documentary opens and closes. For the many messages in the book, Magubane received the Coretta Scott King Award for illustrations. His "acceptance speech" was a series of slides sent from South Africa and presented in absentia at the award breakfast.

HONOR

Bryan, Ashley. *I'm Going to Sing: Black American Spirituals.* Il. **Ashley Bryan.** Vol. Two. Atheneum, 1983. 53 p.

Bryan has spent many hours in the research of African American history in subject areas from folklore and legend to poetry and music. With a concern for making spirituals accessible and meaningful to young people, he designed and illustrated this second volume using woodblock images reflecting the "spirit of the early religious woodblock books." With special skill, Bryan includes facial expressions and depictions of body movements in the pictures to reflect the mood of each of the songs—which range from hopeful, to longing, to joyful and triumphant. In what the artist describes as a desire for "visual unity," with what must have been a technique that required unbelievable patience, he carved the notes using the same woodblock style as the illustrations. The Coretta Scott King Jury was impressed not only with the words and music, but with the fact that the notes all had to be cut in reverse so that when printed they would come out correctly! In selecting this title for illustration honors the committee agreed that now more young people were surely . . . *going to sing.*

Caines, Jeannette. *Just Us Women.* Il. **Pat Cummings.** HarperCollins, 1982. 32 p.

The text is simple and very positively feminine. Aunt Martha is taking her young niece to North Carolina in her new convertible. The trip is to be made with "No boys and no men, just us women." Cummings captures the joy of the trip in two-tone color illustrations that extend the text. One sees a small picture of shoe boxes overflowing with lunch goodies; a double spread shows the fun of roadside shopping; a background of moon and stars completes the picture when the travelers decide to "have breakfast at night." The warmth of companionship is undeniable when at the end of the trip the two "women," with arms around each other, approach the relatives' home at the end of a joyous journey. *Just Us Women* is a rich and positive concept interpreted with artistic skill.

Adoff, Arnold. *All The Colors of the Race*. Il. **John Steptoe**. Lothrop, 1982. 56 p.

Distinguished brown-tone paintings provide the perfect accompaniment to Adoff's free-form poems written from the point of view of a girl born of parents of different ethnic backgrounds—one white, one African American. Steptoe's expressionistic portraits capture the many moods of a young girl searching for identity, respect, and security as she struggles to assert herself in a sometimes-hostile world.

1982   WINNER

Diop, Birago. Trans. and adapted by Rosa Guy. *Mama Crocodile. Maman-Caiman*. Il. **John Steptoe**. Delacorte, 1981. 32 p. (New edition: *Mama Crocodile: An Uncle Amadou Tale from Senegal*. Delacorte, 1982. 32 p.)

When Mother Crocodile warns her children to swim away, they close their ears. Only later, when it's almost too late, do they realize the truth in her words. Steptoe's breathtaking abstract illustrations are appropriately presented in a spectrum of underwater colors to create a strong sense of place while at the same time allowing for interpretation of symbolic history in this cautionary Ovolof tale from West Africa.

HONOR

Greenfield, Eloise. *Daydreamers*. Il. **Tom Feelings**. Dial, 1981. unp.

To "read" *Daydreamers* is to first study closely the faces of the children brought sensitively to life by the artist Feelings. Chocolate brown, charcoal gray, and sepia outlined figures of children speak determination, self-confidence, and a strong feeling that they are a part of the future. There is a message in the set of the jaw of some of the young men remembering their history and "drawing strength from the spirit of their ancestors."

Is it the placement of hand on hips that shouts, "I am somebody"? One wonders what thoughts are going through the mind of the toddler pensively sucking on a tiny finger. A study of the eyes of some of the children—eyes looking into the future—seems to reflect Greenfield's words, "daydreamers letting the world dizzy itself without them. . . ." From toddler to young adult, Feelings's illustrations proclaim that "dreaming has made them new."

Feelings's illustrations have more than an aesthetic visual impact. There is a message of ethnic pride and cultural strength that is totally integrated with Greenfield's poetic text.

1981   WINNER

Bryan, Ashley. *Beat the Story Drum, Pum-Pum*. Il. **Ashley Bryan**. Atheneum, 1980. 70 p.

The striking force of Bryan's lusty woodcut technique had instant appeal for the Coretta Scott King Jury that selected this collection of tales based on Nigerian folklore. There is a rhythm in the curve of the animals' bodies that captures the rollicking beat and humor of Bryan's storytelling. Subtle use of a line gives expressions to the faces of the characters in the stories—stories that cover such topics as why the elephant and the bush cow do not get along or a jab at human foibles in the tale of the man who could not keep a wife because he insisted on counting each spoonful of food placed on his plate.

With the serious artist's true concern for "truth," there is a consistency between the setting—the plains of Africa—and the choice of colors. This is particularly discernible in the full-page illustrations that show blends of earth tones—reds, browns, oranges—as one would see in the homeland of these stories.

HONOR

Greenfield, Eloise. *Grandma's Joy.* Il. **Carole Byard.** Philomel, 1980. unp.

Charcoal drawings on creamy paper tenderly express Greenfield's story of Rhondy's attempts to cheer her grandmother who is sadly packing their belongings into boxes as they prepare to move away. Remembering the special closeness they have shared since Rhondy was a little baby finally cheers and comforts Grandmama. The expressiveness of the illustrations brings an immediacy and a loving respect for people struggling against difficult times, pulling the reader into the story and championing the strength of family ties that carry us through. The illustrations honestly portray both the sadness of the story and the glow of joy and love that comforts child and adult.

Zaslavsky, Claudia. *Count on Your Fingers African Style.* Il. **Jerry Pinkney.** Crowell, 1980. 32 p.

In an African marketplace, young readers are introduced to a way of counting based on the system used in some areas of that vast continent. Pinkney gives graphic life to the concept through clear, black-and-white illustrations. Even without color one is able to see the marketplace and sense its busyness. And indeed the absence of color makes very clear the position of the fingers and the movements of the hands that distinguish one number from another. A close study of the uncluttered illustrations in this book can serve as a fun-filled participatory introduction to an element of mathematics in another language.

1980 WINNER

Yarbrough, Camille. *Cornrows.* Il. **Carole Byard.** Coward-McCann, 1979. unp.

As a modern-day grandmother and mama braid their children's hair in cornrows, the three generations share the stories of the braid patterns that are a part of their African heritage. The charcoal drawings with swirling shapes and dramatic closeups present a series of visions, taking the reader to Africa and then presenting a series of distinct portraits of famous black Americans. Shifting from masks and drums to Malcolm X and Rosa Parks, the drawings soften or become crisp as needed. The illustrations of the African carvings impart solidity, while the drawings depicting the joy of dancing flutter with movement. In the series of portraits of leaders and heroes of black America, each person is easily recognizable and appropriately presented. They include Langston Hughes, Malcolm X, and Marian Anderson. No stilted copies of studio portraits here, but vivid people joyous and proudly leading their kin—the very family glorying in their heritage, in the ordinary world of home, storytelling, and braiding cornrows.

1979 WINNER

Grimes, Nikki. *Something on My Mind.* Il. **Tom Feelings.** Dial, 1978. unp.

Tom Feelings captures the essence of Nikki Grimes's "words" in the faces and body language of the inner-city children of whom she writes. The words are often poignant, speaking of the need to belong, the wish to understand "the secrets grownups share," or just to understand grownups. Feelings's charcoal and sepia drawings leave no doubt in the reader's mind of the message of each piece. There is quiet puzzlement on the face of the young lady, for example, who tries to understand the dichotomy of the mother who urges her to hurry into her Sunday best to go to the Lord's house and then emits some telling curses when she bangs her toe! "Why," asks the child, "instead of going to the Lord's house, don't we invite him to visit ours?" Feelings's line drawings are deceptively simple. The beauty of African American features shows in the faces of each of the children portrayed in this thought-provoking collection.

1974 WINNER

Mathis, Sharon Bell. *Ray Charles.* Il. **George Ford.** Crowell, 1973. 32 p.

When Ford did the illustrations for Mathis's *Ray Charles,* little did he know he would be a part of history! Indeed, the drawings in this young reader's biography made Ford the very first illustrator to receive the coveted Coretta Scott King Award plaque and an honorarium.

Ford expresses the joy of Ray Charles's music beginning with the very cover picture—a smiling musician with swaying dancers reflected in his dark glasses. Looking at black-and-white sketches, interspersed with yellow-toned figures, one can follow the talented pianist from his early days when he lost his sight, through the school where he learned to write down his own musical notations, and on to scenes of large audiences enjoying the sounds of spirituals, blues, and jazz.

Selective Biographies

PEARL BAILEY

1918–1990

Pearl Bailey was born in Newport News, Virginia. At the age of four, she moved with her family to Washington, D. C. Her interest in performing on stage began when her brother Bill, a tap dancer, encouraged her to appear in an amateur hour contest at the Palace Theater in Philadelphia at the age of fifteen. A few years later, after winning the amateur contest at the famous New York Apollo Theater, Bailey knew what her life work would be. Her career in show business included a Broadway debut in *St. Louis Woman*, regular appearances at the Village Vanguard, and singing with bands conducted by Cootie Williams and Cab Calloway.

Retiring from show business in 1975, Bailey made several television appearances before her appointment as special adviser to the United States mission of the United Nations.

In 1980 Bailey returned to school, attending Georgetown University where she earned a B.A. degree in Theology in 1985. Among many honors received, Pearl Bailey in 1988 was awarded the Presidential Medal of Freedom by President Ronald Reagan.

JAMES BERRY

1924–

James Berry is known as a distinguished writer of both prose and poetry. Born and raised in a coastal village in Jamaica, West Indies, this award-winning writer now calls England home. He has been honored internationally for writing that is described as "making a great contribution to people of all ages." His interest in multicultural education manifests itself both in his writing and in his personal involvement in programs that focus on this matter. Among his most recent recognitions are the Order of the British Empire, from the United Kingdom, and the 1993 Boston Globe-Horn Book Award for the poignant story of *Ajeemah and His Son* (HarperCollins).

CLARENCE N. BLAKE

1926–

Born in Cottonplant, Arkansas, Clarence N. Blake grew up in Detroit but spent many years in such far-flung places as Fairbanks, Alaska; Klamath, California; and Ubon, Thailand. His education includes a B.S. from Wayne State University, an M.A. in counseling and guidance from Gonzaga University in Spokane, Washington, and an Ed.D. in adult education from George Washington University. Blake traveled extensively as an Air Force officer, recounting that he had traveled to every state in the United States except Oklahoma and every continent except Africa. When not traveling and teaching, Blake relaxes by playing the mandolin and the piano, fishing, and taking photographs.

The impetus for the *Quiz Book on Black America*, developed with Dr. Donald F. Martin, came from observing the lack of knowledge of black history "on the part of blacks and whites in the United States."

CANDY DAWSON BOYD

1946–

Candy Dawson Boyd was born and raised in Chicago, Illinois. She earned her bachelor's degree at Northeastern and Illinois State universities and a master's degree and Ph.D. from the University of California at Berkeley. She teaches at Saint Mary's College in Moraga, California—the first African American to hold a tenured position at that institution. Boyd was named 1992–93 Professor of the Year at the college; in making this selection Boyd was described as a "gifted and passionate teacher, writer, and colleague."

The themes that one can find in many of Dawson's books reflect her activities with the civil rights movement of the 1960s, her association with Martin Luther King Jr., and her experiences as a field worker in the Southern Christian Leadership Conference.

Boyd's first novel, *A Circle of Gold*, received a Coretta Scott King Award Honor recognition. This book was followed by several other novels that speak directly to African American experience for young readers. Boyd lives with her husband, Robert, in San Pablo, California.

ASHLEY BRYAN

1923–

MATTHEW WYSOCKI

Ashley Bryan was born and raised in New York City in what he describes as a "household crowded with parents, five brothers and sisters, three cousins, 100 birds, and lots of music." In his neighborhood people shared stories and family experiences, and it is to this that he attributes his unending passion for books and stories and music. All these interests come together in the volumes of work Bryan has produced, including collections of African American folk tales, music, and poetry—all enriched with scholarly research.

Bryan studied at Cooper Union Art School in New York City and later majored in philosophy at Columbia University. He taught art at Queens College in New York and at Dartmouth College in New Hampshire.

Bryan is prolific in several languages and has traveled throughout the United States and to England, Italy, France, Germany, Spain, and Africa.

In his books of spirituals, poetry, and folk tales, it is Bryan's goal to bring to young and old picturesque yet accurate interpretations of the rich store of African American history. He uses a variety of techniques to fit the illustrations with the text of a book, selecting woodcuts for his book of spirituals, colorful tempera paints for his folk tales set in the Caribbean, and earth color woodblock prints for some scenes for the stories set in Africa.

Since his retirement from full-time teaching at Dartmouth, Bryan lives in Maine and continues his creativity in a variety of art genres: puppetry, painting, sculpture, and writing. He also lectures around the country.

CAROLE BYARD

1942–

PETER PATE

Carole Byard was born in Atlantic City, New Jersey, on July 22, 1942. Her mother died when Byard was very young, and she was raised by her father with the help of a grandmother. Every time art was offered in school Byard would try to take advantage of the opportunity, but she always felt secretive about her own efforts as though her work was something private. During high school a teacher recognized her talent and helped Byard obtain a full-tuition scholarship to an art school in Ohio. Unable to raise the money necessary, she wrote to the school asking if her place could be held until she could earn enough to attend. That dream was never realized, but she did work at a civil service job, enabling her to attend Fleischer Art Memorial in Philadelphia from 1961 to 1963 and then Phoenix School of Design in New York, where she became an instructor. She has also taught for the Studio Museum in Harlem, Metropolitan Museum of Art, New York Foundation for the Arts, Baltimore School of Arts, Maryland Institute College of Art, and Parsons School of Design. She has had many exhibitions in major and alternative galleries across the country, as well as special commissions. In 1971 Byard was a founding member of the Black Artists Guild. She received a grant from the Ford Motor Company to go to Africa in 1972. The trip to Senegal, Ghana, Ethiopia, and Egypt was a moving experience and a strong influence on her work. Her illustrations of children's books have won many awards since her first Coretta Scott King Award for illustration in 1980 for *Cornrows,* written by Camille Yarbrough.

ALICE CHILDRESS

1920–

Alice Childress—playwright, actress, and essayist—was born in Charleston, South Carolina. At the age of five she was sent to live with her grandmother in Harlem, New York. Childress recalls that her life was poor in terms of money but enriched by love, patience, and her grandmother's appreciation of the arts—a love that she passed on to her young granddaughter. After dropping out of school at an early age, Childress "discovered" the public library. She says that she began then to read at least two books each day.

Childress's writing career began in 1940. By 1943 she moved into acting when she became a part of the American Negro Theater. In 1955 she was the first African American woman to receive an Obie Award for her off-Broadway play, *Trouble in Mind,* that spoke out against the stereotyping of blacks.

As Childress writes she focuses on reaching African American youth and offering them hope in the "struggle to survive in capitalist America." In describing her writing, critics acclaim Childress as a master at her craft—known for deft handling of the language.

Married to Nathan Woodward, Childress now lives on Long Island, New York. She had one daughter who died in 1990.

SHIRLEY CHISHOLM

1924–

Shirley Chisholm, the first African American woman to serve in the U.S. House of Representatives, was born in Brooklyn but spent her early years in Barbados living with her grandparents. She returned to the United States to attend high school, graduated from Brooklyn College in 1946, and earned an M.A. from Columbia University in 1952. Intending to devote her life to early childhood education, she taught nursery school, directed two child care centers, and served as a consultant to the day care division of the New York City Bureau of Child Welfare.

Chisholm's encounters with racism and sexism in college and her interest in community organization inspired her involvement in electoral politics. She served in the New York State Assembly from 1964 to 1968 and was elected to Congress in 1968 from the newly created 12th congressional district in Brooklyn's Bedford Stuyvesant section. Although she was fiercely independent and an outspoken critic of the congressional seniority system, she served on such influential committees as Education and Labor and the Rules Committee. As she had in the state assembly, she pioneered progressive programs to support women and the poor. She championed support for education and urban needs, while attempting to limit expenditures for armaments.

In 1972, Chisholm traveled the country campaigning for the Democratic presidential nomination. She appeared on the ballot in twelve state primaries and received 151 delegate votes at the Democratic convention. Retiring from Congress after serving for fourteen years, she has remained active on the boards of groups that support education, health care, urban concerns, and minority and women's rights. Chisholm now lives in Palm Bay, Florida.

WIL CLAY

1938–

CHERYL L. FRANKLIN

Wil Clay, born in Bessemer, Alabama, lives more recently in Toledo, Ohio, where at Macomber Vocational High School he began his art career in the field of commercial art. Over the years he has studied at the George Vesper School of Art in Boston and at the University of Toledo, where he concentrated on art history and sculpture. During a three-month journey to Cameroon, Africa, he focused on learning about beadwork, painting, and woodworking of the Bamileke and Fulani people and how these art forms related to their tribal festivals and life styles. Exhibits of Clay's paintings and sculpture can be found in private collections around the United States, Canada, Cameroon, and Sierra Leone. In downtown Toledo his six-foot bronze-and-steel sculpture of Martin Luther King Jr. entitled "Radiance" was selected as the winner in an international contest sponsored by the Arts Commission of Toledo, Ohio. Clay's illustrations for children's books reveal the joy and humor he feels when painting and sculpting and sharing stories with youthful audiences.

Clay lives in Toledo, Ohio, with his wife and six children.

LUCILLE CLIFTON

1936–

Lucille Clifton, a native of Depew, New York, has carved a distinguished career in the field of literature by writing for both children and adults. The high quality of her poetry has more than once been recognized by the Pulitzer Award Committee, and in 1987 she was one of three finalists. She also has won the Woman of Words Award, was honored by the New York Public Library as Literary Lion 1989, and in 1993 was inducted into the Maryland Women's Hall of Fame. From 1974 to 1985 this talented writer was given the distinction of Poet Laureate of Maryland.

With a major focus in the field of humanities, Clifton has served on Pulitzer Prize Juries and has been a jurist for the National Endowment for the Arts and for the Poetry Society of America. In other areas of writing Clifton has written several children's books and has had stories accepted for publication in *The Atlantic, Redbook,* and *House and Garden.*

As an educator Clifton has been recognized as the Distinguished Professor of Humanities at St. Mary's College of Maryland where she is presently on the faculty. Other teaching has been at George Washington University and the University of California at Santa Cruz.

Widowed in 1984, Clifton has "six adult children and four grandchildren" and presently calls Maryland home.

FLOYD COOPER

1956–

Floyd Cooper was born in Tulsa, Oklahoma, where he graduated from Tulsa Central High School. He earned a bachelor of fine arts degree from the University of Oklahoma at Norman.

Cooper started in the world of illustration by working in an advertising firm; later he illustrated greeting cards for Hallmark in Missouri.

In 1984 Cooper drew his first children's book illustrations for *Grandpa's Face,* an ALA Notable Book.

The Cooper family lives in Parlin, New Jersey.

PAT CUMMINGS

1950–

ALICE NORRIS

Pat Cummings was born in Chicago but as a child in a military family her travels might well let her call the world her home. When frequent moves from school to school precluded making lasting friendships, this talented artist credits her skill with pen, crayons, and imagination as the source of being accepted, even if only temporarily. Those who have met Cummings would be inclined to add—"also her sense of humor." In spite of many moves, Cummings did stay in one area long enough to earn a bachelor's degree from Pratt Institute in 1974.

When Cummings speaks of her art, in the same breath she speaks of the *need* for freedom of imagination, listing as one of her concerns the rigid rules of art she witnesses as she makes school visitations. One can see her putting her philosophy in action in her choice of colors, angles of perspective, and unusual design details. Perhaps this philosophy is most clearly observed in *C.L.O.U.D.S.* with its action in the sky, decidedly different color names, and a protagonist who is believably purple.

Aware of and believing in the growing need for multicultural materials, Cummings is an active member of a newly formed group—The Center for Multicultural Children's Literature, whose goal is to bring new minority authors and illustrators together with their mentors and publishers in a productive setting.

Cummings and husband Chuku Lee live in Brooklyn, presently with a cat named Cash.

OSSIE DAVIS
1917–

Ossie Davis was born in Waycross, Georgia. After spending his early years in the South, Davis journeyed north and attended Howard University where he earned a B.A. degree in 1939. An early project in the field of performing arts was his direction of the show *Cotton Comes to Harlem*. In 1978 he completed the authorship of *Purlie Victorious*, which enjoyed a long run on Broadway before touring the United States. For *Purlie Victorious* and other works, Davis was inducted into the NAACP Images Awards Hall of Fame in 1978. By 1970 Davis and his actor wife, Ruby Dee, were deeply involved in the civil rights movement, working hard to continue the work of Dr. Martin Luther King Jr. Awards for his civil rights activities include the 1975 Actors Equity Paul Robeson Citation "for outstanding contributions in both the performing arts and society at large."

Most recently Davis and Dee have released their recording of a reading of the entire New Testament. They have two daughters and one grandson and presently live in New Rochelle, New York.

ALEXIS DE VEAUX

1948–

Alexis De Veaux, a native of New York City, is an internationally known poet, playwright, essayist, and short story writer. In this wide range of genres she has published in five languages: English, Spanish, Dutch, Japanese, and Serbo-Croatian. One of her earliest children's books was *Na-ni* published in 1973. Written for older readers was *Don't Explain,* her poetic biography of Billie Holiday written in 1980, for which she received her first Coretta Scott King Award. A second children's book, *An Enchanted Hair Tale* (1987)—a fantasy written in poetry—was once again chosen among the winners of the Coretta Scott King Award and was selected to receive the Lorraine Hansberry Award for Excellence in African American Children's Literature in 1991. Among the plays produced by this talented writer are *Circles* (1972), *The Tapestry* (1976), *No* (1981), and *Elbow Room* (1987). Many of these productions were seen at off-Broadway theaters, in regional theaters around the United States, and on television. Among the television productions was a documentary: *Motherlands: From Manhattan to Managua to Africa Hand to Hand* (1986). In addition to writing for viewing and listening, De Veaux's name can be seen as a byline in articles, poetry anthologies, short story collections, and such diverse sources as *Essence Magazine, The Village Voice, Black Feminist Anthology,* and *Buffalo Women's Journal of Law and Social Policy.*

After earning her doctorate in American studies from the State University of New York at Buffalo, De Veaux now serves on the faculty at that university while continuing to juggle a demanding schedule of travel, personal appearances, and, of course, writing.

DIANE DILLON

1933–

LEO DILLON

1933–

PAT CUMMINGS

Diane Dillon was born in Glendale, California, the daughter of a classroom teacher father and a pianist mother. She recalls that her mother encouraged her interest in art over her interest in music because "she could not stand to hear me practice!" After high school Diane Dillon studied at Los Angeles City College and then at Skidmore. Her critical study of art forms and techniques was heightened when she attended the Parsons School of Design and the School of Visual Arts in New York from 1954 to 1958. It is virtually impossible to discuss Diane Dillon the artist without discussing her husband, Leo Dillon the artist, since they met and married in 1957.

Leo Dillon was born in Brooklyn, New York, the son of parents who migrated to the United States from Trinidad in the West Indies. Leo Dillon credits his earliest interest and inspiration to become an artist to a friend and mentor, Ralph Volman, a native of Trinidad. Volman supplied him not only with materials but with constant encouragement.

After a two-year tour of duty with the United States Navy, Leo Dillon attended the Parsons School of Design from 1953 to 1956 and in 1958 the School of Visual Arts. He worked as an instructor at the School of Visual Arts from 1969 to 1977. It was during his years of study at the Parsons School of Design that he first saw the work of an artist whose skill he admired and determined to surpass: The artist was none other than the person who became his wife in 1957, Diane Dillon.

Leo and Diane Dillon are, indeed, inseparable in the artwork they produce. They balance their techniques, creative ideas, and perspective, so that the finished product is truly a piece from two minds working as one. Their award-winning illustrations have used techniques that range, for example, from woodcuts, to waxed pencil on toned paper, to acetate painting on polished wood.

Together the Dillons have won awards in the United States and abroad, including two successive years of receiving the coveted American Library Association (ALSC) Caldecott medal for *Why Mosquitoes Buzz in People's Ears* in 1976 and the African alphabet/information book, *Ashanti to Zulu* in 1977. In their concern to express the "truth" of a culture in their illustrations, the couple have traveled widely to the sites of their themes to capture the flavor and authenticity of the subject matter.

The Dillons' art has been exhibited in the United States at the Brooklyn Museum of Art, the Pentagon, the American Institute of Graphic Arts, and the Museum of Modern Art in New York and abroad at the Bratislava Book Show. Some of their artwork is a permanent part of the Kerlan Collection at the University of Minnesota.

Leo and Diane Dillon live in Brooklyn with their one son, Lee, who is also an artist, and "two cats who adopted us."

ALFRED DUCKETT

1917–1984

Alfred Duckett was born and raised in New York City. His mother was a housekeeper and his father a Pullman porter. Following high school, Duckett began work as a newspaper boy for the *New York Age,* a Harlem weekly. This job marked the beginning of a career in journalism and reporting that included writing for the *Pittsburgh Courier,* Harlem's *Amsterdam News,* and the Johnson Publishing Company in Chicago. Following service in the U.S. Army during World War II, Duckett returned to school and formally studied journalism at Columbia University. His last job was that of operating his own press agency, handling press releases for such noted clients as Mahalia Jackson, Duke Ellington, and Harry Belafonte.

When asked about his collaboration with Jackie Robinson on the book *I Never Had It Made,* for which he won the 1973 Coretta Scott King Award, Duckett said that he looked upon Robinson as a role model whose story needed to be told from all aspects, not just from the perspective of his heroics on the baseball diamond.

Duckett, described as a pioneer press agent, was the father of one daughter.

MARI EVANS

1923–

Mari Evans was born in Toledo, Ohio. After graduate studies at Toledo University, Evans accepted a position as an instructor in black literature and writer-in-residence at Indiana University and Purdue. From 1971 to 1976 she was an assistant professor teaching black literature at Indiana University in Bloomington. At this time she also produced and directed a television program: "The Black Experience." From 1969 to 1970 Evans was a consultant to the Discovery Grant Program for the National Endowment for the Arts.

Recognized as an outstanding poet, novelist, and essayist, Evans also wrote several children's books. One of the more popular ones was the witty and poetic *Jim Flying High* illustrated by Ashley Bryan. Critics describing Evans's writing state that "it subtly interweaves private and public black frustration and dignity with an infectious perception."

WILLIAM J. FAULKNER

1891–1987

William Faulkner might be called a person with a head just full of stories. He was born in 1891 in Society Hill, South Carolina. In his youth, young Faulkner doubted that he would be able to fulfill his educational ambitions. His mother, widowed while the seven children were quite young, had to struggle to keep the family together. But William Faulkner's ambition became known to an itinerant minister—an African prince who helped Faulkner earn his room and board—and his education began to take shape. Starting with training at the Mayesville Educational Institute he went on to earn a doctorate in theology from Chicago Theological Seminary in 1946.

During his long life Faulkner worked with young people in many different capacities and in many parts of the world. He was the first Negro lecturer for the Quaker Schools and student counselor at Fisk University. Faulkner established the first "summer camps for colored boys" in Philadelphia and in Atlanta, where he pastored the First Congregational Church.

Faulkner stated that he had heard stories just about all of his life. Many of the stories in his award-winning *The Days when the Animals Talked* (1977) were learned from a former slave, Simon Brown, a sharecropper who worked on the family homesite.

Up until his death in 1987, Faulkner was continuing scholarly study on African American folklore, including much of the lore of the Edisto and Sea Islanders living off the coast of South Carolina. These people spoke the Gullah language, with which Faulkner was fascinated and academically interested. The study was to be a major publication in the field of African American folklore.

ELTON FAX

1909–

Elton Fax was born in Baltimore, Maryland. His educational pursuits include a B.F.A. degree from Syracuse University in 1931 and study in Bellagio, Italy, on a Rockefeller Foundation Research Center grant in 1976.

Fax taught at Claflin College in Orangeburg, South Carolina, and A&T College in Greensboro, North Carolina, before taking a position with the Harlem Art Center in New York City.

With oil as his special medium, Fax has illustrated several children's books including Georgiana Faulkner's Melindy series: *Melindy's Medal* (1945) and *Melindy's Happy Summer* (1949) and Florence Hayes's *Skid* (1948).

Fax lives on Long Island and serves as writer-in-residence at the Langston Hughes branch library in the Queens public library system.

TOM FEELINGS

1933–

Artist Tom Feelings was born in Brooklyn, New York. A part of his early education includes two years at the School of Visual Arts. After a two-year stint in the United States Air Force where he served as a staff artist for the graphic division of the Third Air Force, Feelings journeyed to Ghana where he worked for two years on *The African Review* and taught illustration to members of Ghana's government publishing house. While living in Guyana, South America, Feelings worked as a teacher and consultant for the Ministry of Education and trained young artists in textbook illustration.

Feelings's focus in art is described in his words:

When I am asked what kind of work I do my answer is that I am a storyteller in picture form who tries to reflect and interpret the lives and experiences of the people who gave me life.

This philosophy can be observed in practice in Feelings's visual touch added to books such as Julius Lester's *To Be a Slave*. He has been honored with the Coretta Scott King Award for the illustrations in *Something on My Mind* and received the Brooklyn Arts Award for *Jambo Means Hello*. *Jambo Means Hello* (1974) and its companion title *Moja Means One* (1971) were each selected as Caldecott Honor Books.

Feelings's second Coretta Scott King Award came in 1994 for the illustrations in *Soul Looks Back in Wonder*. This is marked as the artist's first book done in color throughout. Using a variety of techniques and media, e.g., collage, wallpaper, paint, etc., the illustrations add dramatic impact to poems selected from the works of several African and African American poets.

Feelings now lives in Columbia, South Carolina, where he teaches at the University of South Carolina and continues to work on his epic visual interpretation of the journeys of slaves from Africa to America: *The Middle Passage*.

CAROL FENNER

1929–

Carol Fenner, the oldest of five children, was born in Almond, New York. Most of her childhood was spent between Brooklyn and rural Connecticut. She recalls the hours of pleasure she spent listening to stories told by her aunt, the noted young-adult author Phyllis Fenner.

Fenner's early ambition was to become a poet, but her writings to the present have been storybooks for young readers, including the 1979 Coretta Scott King Award honor book, *Skates of Uncle Richard*.

MR. AMOS FERGUSON

Mr. Amos Ferguson was born in Exuma, the Bahamas. As a young man he moved to Nassau and took a job polishing furniture to support his family. Mr. Ferguson had sketched and drawn since he was a boy but did not attempt painting until he was an adult. He found that he loved making pictures. Today his paintings cover a wide range of subjects.

Mr. Ferguson's first one-person show was held at the Wadsworth Atheneum Museum in Hartford, Connecticut, in March 1985, and it traveled for two years across the United States. A thirty-minute documentary made by Connecticut Public Television on Mr. Ferguson and his work received an Emmy nomination.

After viewing some of Mr. Ferguson's painting set in his tropical homeland, Eloise Greenfield wrote the lyrical poetry that comprises the honor winning words and pictures in *Under the Sunday Tree.*

GEORGE FORD

1936–

George Ford was born in Brooklyn, New York, but spent his early years in Barbados, West Indies. It was there that his early love for art and illustration was nurtured. Ford remembers that his grandmother "could draw like an angel" and encouraged him in his youthful efforts.

On his return to New York, Ford studied art at such varied centers as the Art Student League, Pratt Institute, the School of Visual Arts, and Cooper Union. He also earned a bachelor of science degree from City College of New York. Exhibits of Ford's work were viewed at Brooklyn Museum in the 1971 exhibition, "Black Artists in Graphic Communications." While working as an art director in the advertising field, Ford turned his talents to illustrating books for children. For one of his early works he received the very first Coretta Scott King Award for illustrations in 1974 for drawings in Sharon Bell Mathis's *Ray Charles.*

Ford's current focus in illustrating children's books seems to reflect once again the influence of his grandmother: "Her interest in social concerns and in portraying human characters with dignity rubbed off on me." He proudly shares as examples of this philosophy the books he has done for Just Us Books, such as *Bright Eyes, Brown Skin.*

Ford, Bernette, his wife, and their daughter live in Brooklyn.

JAN SPIVEY GILCHRIST

1949–

The artist Jan Spivey Gilchrist was born in Chicago, Illinois. Her graduate education was at Eastern Illinois University where in 1973 she earned a bachelor of science degree in art education. She holds a master's degree in painting from Northern Iowa University, completing her work there in 1979. With an interest in painting that began in early childhood, Gilchrist states as her philosophy, "I wish always to portray a positive and sensitive image for all children, especially the African American children." In keeping with this position, Gilchrist has many times collaborated with the noted poet Eloise Greenfield in producing fine books of poetry and prose that speak with a positive force for and about the African American family.

Gilchrist has won many awards for her paintings including recognition from the National Academic Artists Association and the Du Sable Museum, which is in charge of the Purchase Award.

The Gilchrist family, husband, wife, and two children, live in a suburb of Chicago.

BERRY GORDY SR.

1888–1978

Berry Gordy Sr. was enormously successful as a businessman and a family man. From his birth to his death he was a living example of the level of achievement that is possible when one sets high goals and works to meet them. Berry Gordy Sr. recorded his life story for his children as he approached the ninetieth year of his life. And this exemplary life was not lost on his family, as represented by his son, Berry Gordy Jr. Gordy Jr., one-time Golden Gloves boxer and later the owner of a small record store, made the Gordy name famous to many Americans. As an entrepreneur in Detroit, Gordy Jr. started the recording dynasty known as Motown. From an eight-hundred dollar loan he developed the venture into a 50 million dollar business that launched the musical careers of such greats as Smoky Robinson, the Supremes, Martha and the Vandellas, and the Jackson Five. As a musician himself, Gordy Jr. composed several pieces, one of the most popular being "You Made Me So Very Happy."

LORENZ GRAHAM

1902–1989

Lorenz Graham may well be called a pioneer in any review of African Americans in the world of publishing. He is credited with being the first African American to have a book published by a major publishing house. Nine years after the novel was completed and after many rejections, Follett accepted the manuscript for *South Town*, an outspoken criticism of racism in the South. This was the beginning of many years of writing in a variety of literary genres.

Graham, who was born in New Orleans, Louisiana, received his higher education at the University of California at Los Angeles and the New York School of Social Work.

It appears that some of the themes of Graham's early writing were influenced by hearing the stories told by his minister father. This is reflected in his biblical series *How God Fix Jonah*, written in the language of the natives of Liberia where he served for many years as United States ambassador. Later books were written in protest of racism in the United States. A prolific writer, Graham contributed to the literary field until a few years before his death at age 87. His last work was a biography of John Brown, completed in 1980.

SHIRLEY GRAHAM

1907–1977

Shirley Graham was born in Indianapolis, Indiana, the daughter of a Methodist minister and homemaking mother. She was educated at Oberlin College, where she received both her B.A. and M.A. With highly regarded musical talent, Graham studied further at New York University, Yale Drama School, and the Sorbonne in Paris, France. She later taught music at both Morgan State and Tennessee State Universities.

Graham recalled that her love of books started early in childhood. She describes books and music as her childhood partners. Out of this partnership, she wrote a children's opera, *Little Black Sambo,* as well as the opera *Tom Tom,* which was performed by the Cleveland Opera Company in 1937.

A review of Graham's writing shows a focus on historical themes, with many of her titles in the field of biography for young readers. In discussing this, Graham said she hoped to inspire young people of minority groups to achieve the same greatness that her heroes did. Certain factors seem to have had a negative effect on Graham's writing career: Because of the controversy concerning Paul Robeson's loyalty to this country, the U.S. State Department in 1953 had all copies of Graham's biography of Robeson withdrawn from the shelves of overseas libraries! Some critics believe, too, that her writing career was shortened by her marriage in 1951 to her mentor and friend, the civil rights activist W. E. B. DuBois, who was often outspoken against the treatment of racial minorities in the United States. Graham and DuBois spent several years in Ghana in the company of political, social, and educational leaders. Among the educators she met was the teacher Julius Nyerere, about whom she wrote in *Julius K. Nyerere: Teacher of Africa,* a 1976 Coretta Scott King Award honor book.

Graham and husband, W. E. B. DuBois, traveled widely in Africa, Russia, and China. It was in Peking, China, that she died in 1977.

ELOISE GREENFIELD

1929–

Born on May 17, 1929, in Parmele, North Carolina, but raised in Washington, D. C., Eloise Little Greenfield has continued to live in the latter city all her life. Her family moved to the D.C. area in 1930, just as the depression was beginning to grip the country. Life was a struggle for the family. They lived with and shared their home with relatives and friends until being accepted to live in Langston Terrace, one of the first housing projects. She was a shy and quiet child, scared of moving. Since everyone was new at Langston that made the newness easier for her. Her family had a whole house (upstairs and down) to themselves, and in the neighborhood a community began to slowly form. This community provided her with a good place to grow up. She studied piano and joined a singing group called the Langston Harmonettes. Music reverberates in her books and poetry, which have won many awards. Greenfield began to write as a young wife and mother while working at the Patent Office. But it wasn't until 1963 that her first work was published, a poem. Several of her picture books have started out as poetry, yet she has also produced excellent nonfiction and novels. She is a member of the District of Columbia's Black Writer's Workshop and has held positions of leadership with that organization as well as membership in several other writing groups. Sharon Bell Mathis inspired Greenfield to use her artistic talents to help build a collection of literature for children. Greenfield's many books in this field attest to her continuing contribution and dedication to providing the best for today's and future generations of African American children.

VIRGINIA HAMILTON

1936–

Virginia Hamilton was born in Yellow Springs, Ohio, in 1936. Her first book for children, *Zeely,* was published in 1967. Since that time her books have won every major award accorded to American writers, including the Newbery Medal, the Boston Globe-Horn Book Award, the National Book Award, and the Coretta Scott King Award. She is a critically acclaimed author who is often credited with having raised the standards for excellence in children's fiction, folklore, and biography. In 1992 she received international recognition when she was awarded the Hans Christian Andersen Medal for her lifetime contributions to the world of children's literature, making her the fifth American to have received this prestigious award since its inception in 1958.

CARLO ONTAL

Hamilton and her writer husband, Arnold Adolff, the parents of two children, continue to live in Ohio.

JOYCE HANSEN

1942–

AUSTIN HANSEN

Born October 18, 1942, in New York City, Joyce Hansen attended Pace University and earned her M.A. in English from New York University. She has taught reading and language arts in New York City public schools, and is currently a staff developer at an intermediate school in the Bronx, and has been a parttime mentor with Empire State College. Her love of books and writing developed at an early age, nurtured by her mother who wanted to be a journalist and her photographer father who shared with her the stories of his West Indian boyhood and Harlem youth. From her father's photographs, Hansen came to see the "beauty and poetry" in everyday scenes, and her first novels for children and young adults, *The Gift-Giver*, *Home Boy*, and *Yellow Bird and Me*, were stories of the real world in which she grew up. Her work also reflects her interest in the Civil War and Reconstruction. In addition to *Which Way Freedom?*, Hansen has written a second novel set in South Carolina, and her first nonfiction book, *Between Two Fires: Black Soldiers in the Civil War*, was published in 1993.

JAMES HASKINS

1941–

James Haskins was born in Montgomery, Alabama, in 1941 and is currently an associate professor of English at the University of Florida in Gainesville. Since the publication of his first children's book in 1970, he has written more than eighty books for young people. He writes exclusively nonfiction, commenting in 1987, "It seems to me that the more you know about the real world, the better off you are, and since there is so much in the real world to talk about, you are better off concentrating on fact rather than fiction." He writes on a wide range of subjects, and he has been cited by the Coretta Scott King Award Committee numerous times for his biographies of African American luminaries and for his work related to African American cultural history.

KRISTIN HUNTER

1931–

Kristin Hunter was born in Philadelphia during the depression years but grew up in New Jersey. Both of her parents were in education—her father an elementary school principal and her mother a music teacher. However, after Kristin's birth, because of a strange state statute, her mother was no longer eligible to teach. Hunter thus explains her only-child status as based on economics rather than biology or choice. Hunter attended the University of Pennsylvania where she earned a B.S. degree in education in 1951. However, her writing career had started much earlier than her formal education. At the age of fourteen she was writing a weekly column for the local black newspaper.

Hunter's first novel, *God Bless the Child*, was written in 1964. But the author states that her greatest inspiration for writing came after her return to Philadelphia where she drew her themes from observing the life of the people in the area of South Street. It was in this setting that she wrote her award-winning *Soul Brothers and Sister Lou*. In addition to receiving the Coretta Scott King Award, the book was recognized by the Council on Interracial Books for Children and the National Conference of Christians and Jews and has been translated into the Dutch language.

Hunter is married to photographer John Lattany and continues to live and work in Philadelphia.

JOESAM.

1939–

When one talks to JoeSam., the listener hears his interest in and empathy for underprivileged children. In reading his biographical notes the roots of this feeling become evident. JoeSam. was born and raised in Harlem, New York. In spite of what he describes as a difficult childhood, JoeSam. persevered, and after high school he attended Columbia University and later earned his doctorate in education and psychology from the University of Massachusetts at Amherst.

JoeSam. is described as a mixed-media painter and sculptor. In examining his work one gets a sense of an artist who at times is making serious social commentary. His style has been characterized as independent, using simple elements and bright colors.

The colors, simplicity of elements, and the telling of a story with rhythmically angular lines surely were among the factors that brought Coretta Scott King Honor recognition to JoeSam. for the art in *The Invisible Hunters.*

ANGELA JOHNSON

1961–

DALE GALGOZY

Angela Johnson is a native of Tuskegee, Alabama. It was here in the setting of a cross-generational family unit that this writer heard stories. Johnson speaks enthusiastically of the influence of the "rich story-telling tradition in the African American culture. It is art, dance, and music all rolled into one. I am lucky to be a part of this proud tradition."

When asked if the protagonist in *Toning the Sweep,* the 1994 Coretta Scott King Award winner, was someone she knew, Johnson replied, "Emily is a pretty free spirit. There are a few things about her that I see in myself, but it was done unconsciously."

This young author has served as a VISTA volunteer in Ravenna, Ohio, at the King-Kennedy Center. She now lives in Kent, Ohio, where she attends Kent University, works in the Kent Head Start program, and continues to write books warm with the understanding of very young children.

JUNE JORDAN

1936–

June Jordan was born in Harlem, New York City. Her parents were immigrants from the British West Indies. Jordan attributes her interest in words to religious influences. As a member of the Universal Truth faith she was taught what was almost a mantra: "declare the truth"— believing that this can be done effectively through words.

As her writing career developed, Jordan's major interest was in writing poetry for children because, as she states, "children are the most vulnerable and the most beautiful." One of her early books, *Who Look at Me,* was published after she was commissioned by the Academy of Poets to complete this blend of art and poetry as part of a project started by Milton Meltzer and Langston Hughes. Jordan was asked to fill the void after Hughes's untimely death in 1965.

Jordan attended Barnard College, taught English at City College in New York, Connecticut College, and Sarah Lawrence. With Terri Bush she directed the Voice of the Children Workshop "mainly for black and Puerto Rican children in Brooklyn, New York."

JULIUS LESTER

1939–

Julius Lester was born in St. Louis, Missouri, but grew up in Nashville, Tennessee. It was in Tennessee where he later received a bachelor's degree in English from Fisk University. He grew up hearing stories from his minister father, and this love of story is reflected in such titles as *How Many Spots Does a Leopard Have?* Other topics were chosen as Lester more and more realized the need for sharing with his children and with other children an accurate record of the life and contributions of African Americans. The power of this concept was recognized when in 1969 Lester's *To Be A Slave* was selected as a Newbery honor book. When this imaginative author wrote his interpretation of the Brer Rabbit stories in a language that told these tales with dignity, an important part of literary history was made accessible and acceptable to a much wider audience.

Although best known for his writing, Lester is a well-respected photographer whose works are on permanent exhibit at Howard University. He is also a talented guitarist.

Lester now lives in Amherst, Massachusetts, and teaches Judaic and Near Eastern studies at the University of Amherst.

LESSIE JONES LITTLE

1906–1986

Lessie Jones Little was born in Parmele, North Carolina. The daughter of William Jones and Pattie Francis Ridley Jones, Little recalls long hours working in tobacco fields and hating the lingering pungent smell of the plants. Her education included attendance at Higgs Roanoke Seminary near Parmele where she had in-depth studies in black history. After graduation from high school, Little spent two years at North Carolina State Normal School, then taught elementary subjects in a school in rural North Carolina.

After a move to Washington, D. C., Little worked as a clerk-typist in the United States Surgeon General's Office.

Although always an avid reader, Little's writing career did not take root until she was sixty-seven years old. Her first book, *Child Times,* is a three-generation family story written in collaboration with her author daughter, Eloise Greenfield. This title was selected as a 1979 Boston Globe-Horn Book Award honor book in the nonfiction category.

Little, the mother of five children, died of cancer in 1986.

PETER MAGUBANE

1932–

Peter Magubane was born in Johannesburg, South Africa. His outstanding career as a photographer began when working for the magazine *Drum* and as a staff member for the *Rand Daily Mail,* the Johannesburg newspaper. Over the years he has been recognized as the major black South African news photographer. *Black Child,* for which he won the 1983 Coretta Scott King Award, was a follow-up to the more adult-oriented photographic essay, *Magubane's South Africa.* His photographs were outspoken criticisms against apartheid. Magubane's latest recorded residence is in Dupkloof, in the black township of Soweto, South Africa.

DONALD F. MARTIN

1944–

Donald Martin was born in Baltimore, Maryland. His early education was in North Carolina where he graduated from Dudley High School in 1962. After receiving a master of arts degree from the University of Akron, Ohio, he earned a Ph.D. from Ohio State University in Columbus, Ohio, in 1973.

Martin's interest in sharing learning experiences with young people is one of the motivating factors as he teaches and is involved in administrative duties at the University of North Carolina at Chapel Hill. A concern for extending student knowledge of African American history was a motivating factor in collaborating with Dr. Clarence Blake on *Quiz Book on Black America,* a book of challenging questions and answers on a variety of topics related to black history.

SHARON BELL MATHIS

1937–

Sharon Bell Mathis was born in Atlantic City, New Jersey. Her extensive education includes a bachelor's degree from Morgan State University in Baltimore, Maryland, a master's in library science from Catholic University of America, and a fellowship for further study at Wesleyan University. During her career she has worked as a special education teacher, an instructor in a Washington, D.C., parochial school, writer-in-residence at Howard University, and media specialist at the Friendship Educational Center.

ALEX JONES

During her distinguished writing career, Mathis has been cited for her contributions to *Ebony, Jr.* magazine; for winning the Council on Interracial Books for Children writers' award for the still popular *Teacup Full of Roses* (1982), and for receiving Newbery honors for *The Hundred Penny Box* (1975). Her young-reader's biography of Ray Charles, which was a Coretta Scott King Award winner, marked the first time an illustrator award was given. This went to the artist, George Ford. Mathis's most recent book is *Red Dog,* published by Viking Children's Books in 1991.

With an endless interest in helping children expand their creativity, Mathis has been a member of the D. C. Black Writers Workshop where she was designated writer-in-charge of the children's literature division. Mathis currently resides just outside Washington, D. C.

PATRICIA C. McKISSACK
1944–

FREDRICK McKISSACK
1939–

Patricia and Fred McKissack, both natives of Nashville, Tennessee, have lived and worked in Missouri since becoming a writing team in 1982.

Patricia McKissack (nee Carwell) was educated at Tennessee State University where she majored in English. Continued study led to a master's degree in children's literature from Webster University. Fred McKissack is also a graduate of Tennessee State University, where the two writers met and married in 1964. One of the major connections in the early days of their getting to know each other was a common love of literature. Although Fred at one time worked as a civil engineer and Patricia taught school, this element of "the book" resulted in their focus on writing volumes of books that give positive messages to all readers about aspects of the black experience.

As a writing team, the couple have concentrated on bringing to light the productive lives of notable African Americans and writing these biographical and historical books at various reading levels. Patricia reports that "Fred does most of the research and I write it up. . . . Fred fact-checks it and messes around with it . . . and we keep doing that until the text is refined."

Patricia and Fred McKissack share office space in a writing center where, with their youngest son, they work on a regular schedule, writing, reading, researching, and completing books while making preparation for a myriad of public appearances.

MARY E. MEBANE

1933–

Born in 1933 in Durham, North Carolina, Mary Mebane graduated from North Carolina College in 1955. She taught English first at the high school level and then at the college level while she earned her doctorate in American literature from the University of North Carolina. Most of Mebane's writing deals with African American life in the South prior to 1960. She has written poetry and plays and is best known for her *Mary: An Autobiography*, a Coretta Scott King Award honor book for writing. In 1983 she wrote a sequel to it, *Mary, Wayfarer* (Viking).

WALTER DEAN MYERS

1937–

Born in Martinsburg, West Virginia, Walter Dean Myers was informally adopted by family and friends after his mother's death. At age three he moved to Harlem with foster parents. In Harlem he attended plays for children at Columbia University, listened to stories at the local public library, and attended summer Bible school at St. James Church (the church that was to become the first home of the Dance Theater of Harlem). Myers learned stories told by his adopted father and grandfather. The talented writer describes school as frustrating because of his severe speech problem. However, an understanding teacher observed his talent for writing poetry and short stories and encouraged him to express himself on paper where the "words came out more easily." In spite of this encouragement, Myers dropped out of high school and joined the army on his seventeenth birthday. After a stint in the army he returned to civilian life with few skills, very little formal education, and a passion for writing. While Myers was working as an employment supervisor for the New York State Department of Labor, he wrote his first short work for children, *Where Does the Day Go?* He entered the manuscript in the competition sponsored by the Council on Interracial Books for Children and won. From 1970 to 1977 he was tradebook editor for Bobbs-Merrill publishing company. During this time he expanded a short story into his first young adult novel, *Fast Sam, Cool Clyde, and Stuff*, which won the Coretta Scott King Award and provided an important confirmation of his commitment to writing as a career. Since 1977 he has worked full time as a free-lance writer. In addition to his four Coretta Scott King Awards, Myers has received a Newbery Honor Book citation for *Somewhere in the Darkness* (1993), two National Endowment of the Arts grants, and a MacDowell fellowship. In 1984 the author received a bachelor's degree in communication from Empire State College. Myers's most recent honor is the 1994 Margaret Edwards Award for major contributions to the field of literature for young adults.

When not writing, Myers finds relaxation as a talented flutist, a skillful photographer, and a browser through rare book stores wherever he may be.

JOHN NAGENDA

1938–

John Nagenda was born and educated in Uganda. He worked in book publishing until he gave it up to become a full-time free-lance writer in 1965. His short stories, articles, and poetry have been published in Africa, Europe, and the United States. *Mukasa* is his first book for children. He is somewhat fanatical about games and even played cricket for Uganda. He has made his home in England since 1966.

LILLIE PATTERSON

Lillie Patterson was raised by her grandmother in Hilton Head, South Carolina. Patterson states that her grandmother, a singer, gave her a sense of the power of words. As a storyteller Patterson used her command of words in developing educational radio and television programs for children. During a long career in the field of education, Patterson has served as library service specialist and chair of the Elementary School Book Reviewing Committee in the Baltimore public school system.

In her writing career, which started in 1962, Patterson concentrated on creating nonfiction material for young readers, especially simple biographies of noted African Americans. Patterson's name will long be remembered as the first person to win the Coretta Scott King Award in recognition of her *Martin Luther King, Jr., Man of Peace*.

MARGARET PETERS

1936–

Margaret Peters was born in Dayton, Ohio, in 1936. Inspired by her parents to dedicate her life to work in the church and in education, she earned bachelor's and master's degrees and a supervisor's certificate from the University of Dayton. As a high school teacher of English and history, she was troubled by the lack of adequate, accurate information on African American history for young people. The goal of her career from that time onward was to enrich the curriculum with information that children needed about the black experience.

Peters inaugurated after-school classes in black history, became a resource teacher in black history in the Dayton public schools, conducted a weekly radio program on African American culture, and introduced the only course in the Dayton schools that focused on black history. Having retired in June 1993, Peters now volunteers in the schools and continues to write and speak about African American culture. She has served on the board of the Dayton chapter of the Southern Christian Leadership Conference and has chaired the Dr. Martin Luther King Jr. scholarship competition, which has helped twenty-six African American students attend college.

Over the years, Peters has been the recipient of numerous local and national awards for her contributions to education, including the Dr. Carter G. Woodson Award from the National Education Association and the National Council of Negro Women's Award for Excellence in Teaching. Peters has served on the Executive Council of the Association for the Study of Afro-American Life and History and is still very involved in volunteer work, stressing sharing information on African American history.

JEANNE WHITEHOUSE PETERSON

1939–

DAVID KAMMER

Jeanne Whitehouse Peterson was born in Walla Walla, Washington. She earned a B.S. degree from Washington State University before traveling to New York to study at Columbia University. At Columbia she earned a master's degree. After further study Peterson received her Ph.D. in American studies from the University of New Mexico in Albuquerque. Whitehouse taught in public schools and served in Malaysia in the Peace Corps.

When asked about her writing, the author responded that the urge to write was a part of her for a long time, but writing the book for which she received the Coretta Scott King Award came from the fact that she wanted to write a book about her sister who was deaf.

At this time Whitehouse is a lecturer in children's literature at the University of New Mexico and is also actively concerned with Native American affairs in the New Mexico area. She spends as much time as possible caring for and enjoying her string of horses.

BRIAN PINKNEY

1961–

Brian Pinkney, an almost newcomer in the field of children's book illustration, continues to gain wider and wider recognition for his work. Born and raised in New York, Pinkney studied art at the Philadelphia College of Art where he earned a B.A. in fine arts. After further study at the School of Visual Arts in New York City, he graduated with a master's degree in fine arts. While accepting the value of his formal education, Pinkney credits much of his artistic strength to growing up in a family where creativity was the norm. When evaluating his early works, Pinkney states that he wanted to be "just like my father," the noted illustrator, Jerry Pinkney.

With personal growth, continued study, and encouragement, Pinkney developed and honed a distinctive scratchboard technique. As a further refinement of the technique he began adding tints of color and lines that gave a new depth to facial expressions. Among the centers where Pinkney's works have been exhibited are The

Schomburg Center for Research in Black Culture and the National Coalition of 100 Black Women Art Show. His illustrations have appeared in journals such as *New York Times Magazine, Woman's Day, Business Tokyo,* and *Ebony.*

Brian Pinkney lives in Brooklyn, New York, with his author-journalist wife, Andrea.

JERRY PINKNEY

1939–

Jerry Pinkney describes his world as a "world full of color" reflecting the tints and shades of the people, the activities, and the neighborhood connections that come from growing up in a black community. Out of this philosophical background the artist states as one of his goals to "depict black folks as naturally and with as much respect as possible." In viewing Pinkney's illustrations the characters portray the individuality within a group—in clothes, hairstyle, skin tones, and community backgrounds.

Pinkney was born in Philadelphia and studied at the Philadelphia Museum College of Art. Over the years his works have been honored by the Art Director's Show, the American Institute of Graphic Arts, the Council on Interracial Books for Children, and the National Conference of Christians and Jews. In addition to being a three-time winner or honor recipient of the Coretta Scott King Award, Pinkney has also received the Carter G. Woodson Book Award and recognition from the New England Book Show.

If best noted for his book illustration, Pinkney has designed several U.S. postage stamps for the Black Heritage Commemorative Series and later served on the U.S. Postal Service Stamp Advisory Committee. He has also designed many record album covers, and his art has been exhibited in many galleries throughout the United States. Pinkney and his wife Gloria, a new writer in the field of children's literature, live in Croton-on-Hudson, New York.

JAMES RANSOME

1961–

James Ransome was born in Rich Square, North Carolina. He recalls a happy childhood under the nurturing love of his grandmother. After a move to New York, Ransome earned a bachelor's degree in 1987 from Pratt Institute, New York City.

In the early days, this talented illustrator earned his living illustrating not only children's books but such items as tote bags, greeting cards, and—closer to his goal of "illustrating more satisfying material"— book jackets for children's novels. Ransome's first book illustrations, for Angela Johnson's *Do Like Kyla,* earned him the Parenting Magazine's Reading Magic Award.

In discussing his approach to illustrating, Ransome says he has been influenced by studying the works of such greats as Cassatt, Sargent, and Degas. Then he says with genuine admiration that he derives great strength and encouragement from artist and illustrator Jerry Pinkney. When asked about the characters in many of his books, Ransome says that he photographs people and uses them as models and that he is now looking forward to including his new daughter, Jamie, in his next picture book.

Ransome, his wife Lesa, daughter Jamie, and their ever-present Dalmatian, Clinton, live in Poughkeepsie, New York.

FAITH RINGGOLD

1930–

Faith Ringgold was born in New York City and was educated in the schools of upper Harlem. Growing up in Harlem during the depression, her family still saw to it that Faith and her brother and sister enjoyed cultural experiences. As a young child Faith showed artistic ability, and her interest in art was further stimulated by frequent trips to the city's art museums.

Along with the usual academic subjects in high school, Ringgold studied art and continued this study in the School of Education at City College, New York, where she earned her bachelor's degree. She spent years teaching art in the city schools, but deep down there was

this call to express something more of her African American heritage and to encourage museum curators to give greater exposure to the art of African American women. From flat paintings, the artist moved to soft sculpture, remembering the faces of her family and the people of her Harlem childhood. With time came another change in her technique: picture stories in acrylic on canvas bordered by quilt squares, which told full quilt stories with details that engrossed the viewer in "reading" every story very carefully. This unique art style has brought renown to Ringgold, and she has recently transposed some of her historical quilt stories into picture books for young readers.

Presently Ringgold, living in New Jersey in sight of the George Washington Bridge, divides her time between teaching as a full professor and pursuing her art.

DOROTHY ROBINSON

1929–

Dorothy Robinson was one of the earliest winners of the Coretta Scott King Award for *The Legend of Africania* in 1975. A librarian in the Chicago Public Library System, the author states that she conceived the idea for her book during the civil rights movement of the 1960s. It was one of many books that she believed were needed to help children of the civil rights era understand what was being seen on television and her "way of explaining to them who they were and the beauty of their history as African Americans."

In 1990 this author-librarian founded a program, "The Genie in Every Child," designed to help parents and teachers use books and reading to raise self-esteem.

Robinson was born in Waycross, Georgia, went to college at Fisk University, and earned her masters in library science from Atlanta University. Today she calls Chicago home.

CHARLEMAE ROLLINS

1897–1979

Charlemae Rollins was born in Yazoo, Mississippi, in 1897. Her early childhood was spent in Oklahoma with her grandmother, a former slave. After teaching in Oklahoma, Rollins moved to Chicago where she began her career as a librarian in the public library system. It was the start of an outstanding career as a children's librarian—with programs that moved beyond the traditional story hours and reading guidance activities. In circulating material to the children, she became acutely aware of the shortage of cultural material that spoke positively of the black experience. With this observation, Rollins turned her talents to writing criticisms decrying racial stereotyping and also writing quality biographies about blacks who had made outstanding contributions to American culture while overcoming tremendous obstacles. Rollins was one of the first editors of the National Council of Teachers of English (NCTE) bibliography *Reading Ladders of Human Relations*, which addressed the recognition of the importance of cultural diversity.

For this pioneer in service for children the awards were many. Rollins was the first black to be given life membership in the American Library Association, after becoming the first black to serve as president of the then Children's Services Division; she earned the American Brotherhood Award of the National Conference of Christians and Jews, the Grolier Foundation Award, and the National Centennial Award, to name a few.

Within the American Library Association, the name Charlemae Rollins has a permanent place in the Division of Association for Library Service to Children through the annual Charlemae Rollins President's Program.

ELLEASE SOUTHERLAND

1943–

Ellease Southerland, a native New Yorker, was born in Brooklyn. She attended Queens College and later earned a masters of fine arts degree from Columbia University. Growing up as the oldest of fifteen brothers and sisters in a close-knit family, Southerland recalls a household organized on the religious principles of her minister father. She remembers it, too, as a house filled with music. The author relates that the religious motifs that permeate her first novel, *Let the Lion Eat Straw*, are based loosely on the home life she knew. She also states that the mother figure in the novel is a bittersweet reflection of her mother. A sequel to her first novel, *A Feast of Fools*, appeared in *The Anthology of Contemporary African-American Fiction* (1990).

The major focus of Southerland's writing has been poetry. Her works have been published in several periodicals including *Black World*, *The Massachusetts Review*, and *The Journal of Black Poetry*. The high quality of her work won her the Gwendolyn Brooks Poetry Award in 1972.

Southerland is an adjunct professor at Pace University and lives in Jamaica, New York.

JOHN STEPTOE

1950–1989

John Steptoe was born in Brooklyn, New York, in 1950. From the time he was an art student in high school, he knew that he wanted to create picture books for African American children. His first book, *Stevie* (Harper, 1969), was published when he was just nineteen, and it met with immediate success when the book was reprinted in its entirety in *Life* magazine, calling this talented young artist to national attention. His early style was often compared to that of French painter Rouault, and through the years his picture books showed the development of a painting style that experimented with abstraction, expressionism, and surreal-

ism. Steptoe's tragic death in 1989 cut short a career filled with vision and promise. In his brief lifetime he won numerous awards and distinctions, including two Caldecott Honor Awards, the Boston Globe-Horn Book Award, and numerous Coretta Scott King Awards. The legacy John Steptoe left to children and children's literature is perhaps best summed up in a statement he made about his work in 1988: "In my picture books I put all the things I never saw when I was a child."

RUTH ANN STEWART

1942–

Ruth Ann Stewart was born in Chicago. She attended the University of Chicago but completed her studies at Wheaton College in Massachusetts, where she earned a bachelor of arts degree in 1963. After earning a master of science degree from Columbia University in New York, she did further study at Harvard University and, in 1987, at the Kennedy School of Government.

Stewart has served on several advisory boards including the Board of Visitors at the Pittsburgh School of Library and Information Science, the Board of Trustees at Wheaton College, and the District of Columbia Historical Records Advisory Board.

In writing *Portia*, the book for which she won Coretta Scott King Award honors, Stewart stated:

> It was my intention to tell the story in an interesting and lively manner of a woman whose life also provided a previously unknown perspective on an important chapter in African American history. . . . Even though Portia was the daughter of a famous man [Booker T. Washington], her career and personal struggles are common to the stories yet to be written of many black women. . . . It is my hope that this literary shortcoming will be vigorously addressed and there will be many Portias (including a few more of mine) taking their place on shelves of libraries and bookstores in the near future.

Stewart lives in Washington, D. C., and has one daughter.

MILDRED D. TAYLOR

1943–

JACK ACKERMAN

Mildred Taylor was born in 1943 in Jackson, Mississippi, but her father soon moved his young family North because he did not want his daughters to grow up in the segregated South. Taylor showed promise as a writer early on when she won first prize in the Council on Interracial Books for Children contest in 1973 with a fictionalized story from her father's childhood in rural Mississippi. The award-winning manuscript, *Song of the Trees,* was published by Dial in 1975 and became the first in a series of books Taylor would write about the Logan family. It was also awarded the first of many honors she would receive from the Coretta Scott King Award Committee. Her second book, *Roll of Thunder, Hear My Cry* (Dial, 1976), won the Newbery Medal, was a National Book Award finalist, was a Boston Globe-Horn Book honor book, and was a Coretta Scott King honor book. She has continued the Logan family saga in subsequent books, firmly establishing herself as one of the premiere writers of American historical fiction for children and adolescents. She focuses almost exclusively on her father's era because she wants to bring to life for contemporary children the importance of the previous generation's experiences and work in laying the groundwork for the civil rights movement of the fifties and sixties.

Taylor makes her home in Boulder, Colorado.

JOYCE CAROL THOMAS

1938–

Joyce Carol Thomas was born in Ponca City, Oklahoma, one of nine children. Among her childhood memories is that of picking cotton in fields near her home. A less-backbreaking job came later when she worked as a telephone operator by day while attending night classes at San Jose University in California. At San Jose she earned a bachelor's degree in Spanish. Her master's in education came from Stanford University.

As an educator, Thomas has taught in middle schools, high schools, and universities, including serving as associate professor in the English department at Purdue University. She also taught classes in creative writing at the University of California at Santa Cruz. In addition to her teaching, Thomas has traveled as a lecturer in Africa, Haiti, and the United States.

Thomas has earned several awards and honors for her writing in such diverse genres as poetry, short stories, novels, and plays for both adults and young adults. *Marked by Fire,* one of her earliest novels for young adults, was selected as one of the titles to be included in the American Library Association's Best Books for Young Adults in 1982. This talented author has also received critical acclaim for an anthology of short stories that she edited: *A Gathering of Flowers: Short Stories about Being Young in America* (1990). When asked about her most recent publication, the Coretta Scott King honor book, *Brown Honey in Broomwheat Tea,* Thomas recalls, "In just about all my novels, broomwheat tea is steeped, poured, sipped. When I had a headache or caught chicken pox . . . my mother would go into the weed fields and pick the tea leaves and serve me a steaming cup from the crushed blossoms." Readers of this book of lyrical poetry will take comfort in Thomas's mother's assertion as the tea is being sipped, "Good for what ails you."

Thomas, currently a professor of English at the University of Tennessee, is the mother of four and the grandmother of six. She lives just outside Knoxville, Tennessee.

JANICE MAY UDRY

1928–

Janice May Udry was born in Jacksonville, Illinois, a small town that she describes as earning a place on the map because it was the center for the construction of Ferris wheels. This writer, who wanted to write "ever since I learned how to read," earned a B.S. degree from Northwestern University. After her marriage she moved to Chapel Hill, North Carolina. Some of the ideas for her books came from observing the spontaneous excitement that came from sharing quality picture books with young children. This was most evident when she worked as an assistant in a nursery school. Udry is the author of the 1957 Caldecott winning book *A Tree Is Nice*. Her book *The Moon Jumpers* was a Caldecott honor book in 1960.

MILDRED PITTS WALTER

1922–

Mildred Pitts Walter, born in De Ridder, Louisiana, received her bachelor's degree in English from Southern University in New Orleans. She earned a master's degree in education after studying in California and completing her work at the Antioch extension in Denver. With her educational background, Walter taught school in California, served as a consultant at Western Interstate Commission of Higher Education in Denver, Colorado, and later was a consultant teacher and lecturer at Metro State College.

The writer inside Walter saw her close her teaching career in 1969 to devote all of her time to writing. Her dedication to sharing African American history with young readers can be seen in some of her prize-winning books: *Because We Are*, which takes a provocative look at school integration, and *Mississippi Challenge*, a scholarly study of that state's history from the African American perspective.

Walter has been active in a variety of civil rights movements and involved in pursuits in search of worldwide peace. At the time that she won the Coretta Scott King Award for *Justin and the Best Biscuits in the World,* the award was accepted in absentia because the author was a delegate with a group on a peace mission to Russia. Before her husband's death the couple traveled widely for civil rights causes around the United States and abroad in Africa and China.

Mildred Pitts Walter, the mother of two sons, makes her home in Denver, Colorado.

KATHLEEN ATKINS WILSON

1950–

Artist Kathleen Wilson grew up in Ypsilanti, Michigan. Her formal art training began at Pepperdine University and the Otis Art Institute in Los Angeles.

Wilson's art reflects her philosophical approach to the subject—that of sharing her heritage through "artistic symbolism." Her major focus is that of using silhouette figures set against luminous backgrounds and of each picture celebrating some aspect of her African American heritage while inviting others to join in the celebration. She uses as her media watercolor, wax crayon, oil, and opaque black, the combination of which results in art that has been described as "magical."

Soft-spoken, serious, yet warm and friendly, Wilson speaks of the spirituality that is the driving force in all that she does. The parents of two children, Kathleen and her business-manager husband now live in Hawthorne, California.

INDEX

Rita Auerbach is school library media specialist in Port Washington, Long Island. Her service for ALA includes membership on the Coretta Scott King Award Jury for a three-year term and the present coordinator and program director of the Storytellers' Discussion Group.

Carol A. Edwards grew up in Colorado but spent an exciting part of her life in Botswana, Africa. Currently employed as children's librarian in the Minneapolis public library system, Edwards has served on the Coretta Scott King Award Task Force and Jury. She is a reviewer for the *School Library Journal* and has been a staff member for the Cooperative Children's Book Center, University of Wisconsin at Madison.

Kathleen Horning is a children's librarian at Madison, Wisconsin, public library as well as librarian and coordinator of special collections at the Cooperative Children's Book Center, University of Wisconsin, Madison. Horning is the editor of *Alternative Press Publishers of Children's Books*. With Ginny Moore Kruse she coauthored *Multicultural Literature for Children and Young Adults* and was a contributor to *Multicolored Mirror: Cultural Substance in Literature for Children and Young Adults*. Horning has been a member of the Coretta Scott King Award Jury.

Ann Miller is a graduate of Nova University, Ft. Lauderdale, Florida, where she received a degree in psychology. She then earned her master's in library science from the school of library and information science at the University of South Florida, Tampa. Miller is presently branch librarian in the Broward County public library system. Her ALA contributions include a recently completed term on the Coretta Scott King Award Jury.

Henrietta M. Smith is Professor Emerita on the faculty of the school of library and information science, University of South Florida, Tampa, where she continues to teach in the area of materials for children and young adults. She has served on Newbery, Caldecott, Batchelder, and Wilder Award committees and has chaired the Coretta Scott King Task Force and served on the Award Jury.